Springboard ®

WOMEN'S DEVELOPMENT WORKBOOK

developed and written by

Liz Willis and Jenny Daisley

HAWTHORN PRESS

Published by Hawthorn Press, Hawthorn House, 1 Lansdown Lane, Lansdown, Stroud GL5 1BJ, UK
Tel: 01453 757040 Fax: 01453 751138 Email: info@hawthornpress.com Website: www.hawthornpress.com

Cover design by Francis Porter
Typeset by Hawthorn Press
Printed by Butler Tanner and Dennis, Frome, Somerset

First edition 1990, reprinted 1991
Second edition 1992, reprinted 1993, reprinted 1994
Third edition 1995, reprinted 1996
Fourth edition 1998, reprinted 1999
Fifth edition 2000, reprinted 2001, reprinted 2002, reprinted 2004 with updates, reprinted 2005, reprinted 2006
Sixth edition 2008, reprinted 2008, reprinted 2010

Acknowledgements
Natasha Josefowitz for her kind permission to use her verse Support Systems from her book Is this where I was going? published by Columbus Books 1986. Sheldon Press for their kind permission to quote from part of Allan Pease's book Body Language 1981. The Training Agency, as it was, for their permission to use Valerie Hammond and Dr Margaret Ryan's material in Power and Influence in Organisations. Illustrations by Viv Quillan on pages 41, 100, 162, 165, 219.

By the same authors
Developing Women through Training 2002 The Springboard Consultancy
The Assertive Trainer 2004 The Springboard Consultancy
Women Singled Out 1995 The Springboard Consultancy
Personal Development has Legs 2006 The Springboard Consultancy

ISBN 978-1-903458-74-7

Contents

CONTENTS

Getting in touch

You can work through this book on your own. However, it is also designed to be used as part of the Springboard Women's Development Programme, which will give you the support of other people and short workshops to help you get the best out of this book. Get in touch with us to receive the list of licensed Springboard trainers in your area or check our website for trainers and courses.

There is also the Springboard Newsletter – 'NewsSplash' – which provides information for anyone interested or involved in Springboard, whether you are an individual, an employer or representing an organisation. Contact us for details of 'NewsSplash' or download it from the website.

Many Springboard programmes are run inside organisations. Only trainers trained by us are licensed to run Springboard programmes. Contact us for further details about how to implement a Springboard programme in-house, or about how to become a licensed trainer. There is also Navigator, a parallel programme for men's development.

We look forward to hearing from you. To get in touch email us or use the form on the next page.

The Springboard Consultancy,
Holwell, East Down, Barnstaple, Devon, EX31 4NZ, UK
Tel: 01271 850828 Fax: 01271 850130
E-mail: office@springboardconsultancy.com
www.springboardconsultancy.com

Tick the box(es) which apply to you.

I would like information on:

- ☐ local licensed trainers as I am interested in attending a Springboard programme
- ☐ becoming a freelance licensed trainer
- ☐ licensing in-house trainers
- ☐ having a Springboard programme run in my organisation
- ☐ Navigator – the men's programme
- ☐ programmes for women managers
- ☐ programmes for older workers
- ☐ programmes about creativity and innovation
- ☐ the research report 'Personal Development has Legs' about the longer term results of personal development training
- ☐ I would like to be put on the 'NewsSplash' mailing list

Name   Date

Job Title (if applicable)

Organisation (if applicable)

Address

                                                 Postcode

Daytime Tel. No.

Evening Tel. No.

About the authors

Liz Willis and Jenny Daisley are well known as two of the UK's leading women's development consultants. In addition to their training and consultancy work, they have also written extensively on women's development and personal development generally.

Both highly respected as consultants in their own right, they collaborated in designing and developing the three month Springboard Women's Development Programme which first won the Lady Platt Award for the most innovative Equal Opportunities training and also a prestigious government awarded National Training Award. Several organisations have also used the Springboard Programme as part of their strategy on women's development, which has won them Opportunity Now awards. This workbook is an essential ingredient of the Springboard Programme.

Since the first publication of this Workbook, Liz and Jenny have delivered an extensive programme of training and licensing other trainers to use the Springboard Programme and Workbook. This has resulted in an international network of over 850 Springboard trainers delivering Springboard programmes in the UK, USA, Denmark, Poland, Australia, New Zealand, France, Ghana, South Africa, Spain, India, Finland, Austria, Sweden, the Republic of Ireland, Saudi Arabia, Kenya, Tanzania, Malawi, Kuwait, Armenia and Malta, with special editions of the Workbook being translated and culturalised for most of these countries.

Liz and Jenny draw on many experiences of working in depth with women from all the countries in which Springboard is now running, as well as other women's development work in Eastern Europe. The main mission of their business, the Springboard Consultancy, is to provide access to good quality development training to women and men from diverse backgrounds and circumstances. Having started their careers at the bottom of organisations and worked their way up, they have personally experienced many of the hurdles encountered by women, both at work and in their personal lives.

Liz and Jenny have also written 'Developing Women Through Training', 'Women Singled Out', 'Personal Development has Legs' and 'The Assertive Trainer' and have co-written *Navigator,* the 'brother' book on men's development, with James Traeger.

In 2000 they were made European Women of Achievement for developing pan-European understanding and inspiring others. They have also successfully developed the programmes Spring Forward for managers, Fresh Steps for older workers, and Liz works with creativity and innovation on The Purple Process programmes which she designed.

Thanks

When the first edition of Springboard was published it was a new and unprecedented idea and we were curious about how it would be received. Now we are approaching 200,000 copies having been sold, there are special editions in other countries and it is available in Braille and on tape. This achievement is due entirely to the enthusiasm and commitment of many people. We've been delighted with the overwhelmingly positive reaction to the book and are also grateful for the constructive criticisms and helpful suggestions we've received. In particular we want to thank:

The network of licensed Springboard trainers. When the first edition was published there were just two of us – now there are over 800 and many of the changes in this latest edition have come from helpful conversations with other Springboard trainers, including Amanda Rowan who contributed her image diagram on page 222.

Rachel Bristow, Elisabeth Winkler, Gaye Mallows, Shereen McQuoid, Lullyn Tavares, Sue Matthews, Tina Henderson, Judith Secker, Anita McGeough, Rachael Gilbert, Lorna Jackson and Naseem Aboobaker who wrote up their life stories. These stories and quotes bring to life the issues raised in the book. We admire the generosity of these women who are prepared to be visible so that others can learn from their experiences.

Julie Spence, OBE, for contributing the Foreword. She has championed women and their development and encouraged many women in police services to benefit from the Springboard programme, amongst her many other activities to support women.

At Hawthorn Press, Martin Large who believed in the book enough to publish it, Rachel Jenkins for her warmth and support in managing the book production generally, and this edition in particular, and Frances Fineran for the design and layout of this edition. Francis Porter for the cover design and Viv Quillin for her illustrations.

Special thanks to all our Springboard Consultancy office colleagues for their cheerful and practical support of us and the network of Springboard colleagues, especially Pat Glover who has contributed greatly to this new edition and advised us on the more literary aspects.

All the people at the BBC who were involved in their Women's Development Programme, the predecessor to Springboard, in particular Jacqui Kasket, now a freelance consultant, and Bob Nelson, then Head of Corporate Management Development.

Tens of thousands of women in 21 different countries have now completed Springboard programmes, so we welcome you to the opportunity to benefit from their ideas and experiences as you work through it for yourself.

Liz Willis and Jenny Daisley
August 2007

Foreword

I am delighted to commend this new and updated Springboard workbook to you. I first came across the Springboard Women's Development Programme, and an earlier edition of this workbook, as I moved into a senior management position and was looking for something that would enable the latent and often suppressed talent of women in policing to come to the fore and add real value to policing.

Subsequently, in my capacity as President of the British Association for Women in Policing, I was part of reviewing the needs of women in the Service and developing 'The Gender Agenda'. This was published in 2001, and recommended actions for Police Services across the UK to take to maximise the potential of their women staff. In that we cited the Springboard programme as being one of the most positive initiatives available for women in the Service.

Over the years, and while working in three police services, I have consistently seen the benefits that women gain from participating in the Springboard Programme. The core of the programme is individual women working through this workbook, which remains private to them. I see the tangible results, not only when I meet the women on programmes, but also in my day-to-day work with women who have benefited from this workbook. Women think about themselves and life in a more positive and confident way and create solutions, not problems.

Visiting Springboard Programmes is an uplifting experience; the energy and enthusiasm is tangible. My vision and the reason I invested in Springboard (and the Navigator programme for men) was to enable individuals to unlock their potential and really see what they are capable of achieving; and then set themselves on a path to achieve it. There is evidence that the investment is paying off – it is now up to the individuals to build on this start whilst being supported by their organisation. Many successful women in policing, in terms of both personal and professional achievement, are graduates of the Springboard Programme.

So I urge you to work through this workbook, and to do the exercises even when you are not sure why you are doing them, because they are all there for a reason, even if it is just to raise your awareness. Whether you are in paid employment or not, you can only benefit from the opportunity this workbook gives you to pause, look at your life, make conscious decisions and then take action on them to carve out a fulfilling future for yourself.

Ultimately your life is what you, not anyone else, makes of it and living it to the fullest, being the best that you can be and contributing to your community will both make a difference to you and the world a better place.

Julie Spence OBE
Chief Constable, Cambridgeshire Constabulary
President of the British Association for Women in Policing

This is it! There are no rehearsals or preparations. Your life is on and running.

T. Powell

Begin It Now!

Objectives
- to get you off to a good start
- to start collecting the information you need

This chapter is important because

- how you begin will influence how much you get out of the programme
- channelling your energy enables you to get the best out of yourself
- it represents a golden opportunity

Contents
- our approach
- working with this workbook
- information is power!
- meditation and relaxation
- dealing with change
- your objectives
- the luck challenge
- summary and action
- profile of Rachel Bristow

Are you a starter, a runner or a finisher? Beginning well will influence how much you get out of Springboard. Channelling your energy into working through the workbook means you get the best out of yourself. So begin well now!

You are faced with a golden opportunity. Whether you are tackling this workbook on your own or with other people, you have already taken the first step by opening this book and starting. You have either created, or grabbed, the opportunity!

Springboard is all about what you can do for yourself. It's not about what your family should do for you, what the government, your partner, your colleagues, your manager, or your organisation should do for you. You change what you want to change and be who you want to be. You decide which boundaries you want to keep, which you have to keep and which to shift or eliminate completely.

It's about you accepting the responsibility for yourself, realising that no one hands you life on a plate, making the most of everything you've done so far and, looking the world in the eye, believing 'I can do this'.

It is also an unusual opportunity as most of us don't set aside regular chunks of time to think about ourselves and make positive changes in our lives. You may have decided to do this for yourself, or you may have been encouraged and subsidised by your employer to do so; either way, give yourself a real chance and make the most of it!

More than just a workbook, Springboard is a complete development programme which you can work through superficially or in as much depth as you want. Also it can be done in lots of different ways such as:
- with workshops in a Springboard Women's Development Programme
- by yourself
- with a few friends
- in support or networking groups

Springboard

- results in practical action
- is about making changes that are appropriate to your life and your circumstances now
- isn't a career directory
- is about you developing yourself as a whole person
- requires you to be self-motivated and committed
- requires energy and enthusiasm
- can be done in a superficial manner, very deeply, and every other way in between!
- puts responsibility for your development clearly with you
- lets you decide what to do with your life
- doesn't contain any magic answers!

Our approach

This book has been developed and written for all women currently in or thinking about being in employment: women who are not at the top of their organisation i.e. most working women. So this book is for you, whether you're:

- working part-time or full-time
- working freelance
- considering a return to work
- starting out on your career
- approaching retirement
- not looking for paid work but keen to stretch yourself
- coping with redundancy
- thinking of setting up your own business
- just promoted
- in academic life and needing to reassess your goals
- in management and wanting to review and re-plan
- or whatever!

Where do you think you are you at the moment? Are you:

- at a new beginning taking the first steps?
- in a comfortable rut?
- at a crossroads wondering which way to go?
- at the top of a hill, surveying the view and wondering 'What now?'
- discovering that the path you are on is a cul-de-sac?
- in a Rolls Royce purring along?
- in an old banger that may give out at any time?
- going in totally the wrong direction?
- soaking your feet in a bucket of water and hoping the pain will go away?
- out of breath and watching others go by?
- on a superb plateau going nowhere?
- having fun, hoping it will last for ever and knowing it won't?
- trudging along and doing OK but welcoming a bit of company on the way?

Wherever you are, you have this workbook because you are a woman wanting to change something.

The content and process of the book is very broad, to encompass women of all ages, in all stages of their lives, of all races, all levels of ability and disability and with all levels of qualifications. The approach is also broad enough to take in the vast array of women's circumstances.

We refer to 'partner' throughout as the close permanent relationship in your life, if you have one. If you're thinking of setting up your own business, of course, you may also have a business partner. We use the word 'work' throughout to mean wherever and however you work. This covers paid, unpaid and voluntary work.

The approach is based on our fundamental beliefs about women's development:

- you can develop yourself more fully, no matter what your circumstances
- you have to want to do it or at least have a sense of questioning where you are now
- you are capable of taking more control over your life
- developing your whole self develops your work life

- women still do not always have the opportunities they want to have in a world that has been structured and controlled by men
- small, practical steps work
- the answers lie in the practical experiences of women, both at work and at home
- women develop, achieve and work in a way which is different from men's way
- development can be a difficult process – that's why you have to want to do it
- you can do it – if you want to

We also believe that development, although always challenging and often painful, is enormous fun and leads to greater fulfilment and happiness; so we hope that it will be enjoyable for you, as well as challenging!

 There are four kinds of people in the world:
People who watch things happen,
People to whom things happen,
People who don't know what is happening,
And people who make things happen.

Anon.

Working with this workbook

In this workbook you can do a substantial review of your life, where you are, where you want to be and how to bridge this gap. Work through the chapters in the order they are given unless you are feeling particularly stressed at the moment then jump to Chapter 9 or, if you are applying for a new job, then leap to Chapter 11! This is your workbook so:

- work through all of it – everything is there for a reason
- keep it safe and private unless you want to show someone
- work through it in line with the Springboard Women's Development Programme if you are attending one. This means devoting about three hours per week over three months

- treat the workbook as a course and participate in all the bits: inputs, exercises, action points
- decide what you will clear from your diary to make space for you

The workbook flows from looking at yourself and the world about you in the early chapters through to setting goals and working to achieve them in the later chapters. At the end of the workbook there are useful sources of information and support and also your **personal resource bank** which will help you over and over again find the information you need to help you apply for jobs/roles, reset goals or make changes in your life.

Pages with ✳ are marked so that you can photocopy them before you write on them (pages 80-82 and 218) or give them to other people to complete.

Information is power!

You may need more information or you may have too much. With more and more information available on the internet there is a danger of being swamped! Gaining information can increase awareness, minimise risks, give you confidence, energy, ideas and power; looking for information can let people know that you are interested in a topic. If you tend to rush into things without much information, get yourself informed and, if you have too much information, experiment with combining your intuition with fewer facts.

There are a few starter websites on page 313-315. Keep up to date with search engines, look at blogs and generally explore. If you are employed make sure that you are familiar with your organisation's intranet and all the resources available internally. If computers and the internet are unfamiliar to you then get yourself on a course or get a teenager to show you the basics.

Don't forget to use libraries, books, leaflets, newspapers and magazines. While you are working through Springboard, experiment with reading different material from your usual books, magazines or newspapers or explore a friend's favourite websites for a change.

Get your antennae working so that you spot different information and sources of support or advice to help you set and achieve your goals!

People to help you

Later in the workbook you will look in more detail at the people who may help you. Most people will be helpful if you ask them for information or support, particularly if you explain that you are working through Springboard. Ask for information, advice, ideas and other contacts. At the end of each chapter there are real stories from other women which may give you ideas and inspiration.

Meditation and relaxation

Each chapter also has a short meditation or relaxation exercise that you can do each evening or morning to focus your mind for the days or weeks that you are working on that chapter. If you follow a particular path of meditation then use that one. If you don't, simply sit or lie down where you won't be disturbed and allow yourself to relax. Close your eyes or lower them to look at the floor and breathe deeply by breathing out a little bit extra. If you notice that you can count to two or three as you breathe in then count double that amount to four or six as you breathe out. Do that three times and then let your breathing settle. Then start the meditation. It could take you two minutes or 10. That is up to you. These meditations are meant to be positive and helpful so, as a health warning, if you find yourself getting negative or having unpleasant thoughts then take control and either change the thought or open your eyes and bring yourself out of the meditation.

MEDITATION

The meditation for this chapter is to picture yourself in a pleasant scene in nature: a beach, a meadow, a wood or wherever. Allow yourself to really take in the scene. In the comfortable relaxation of that pleasant scene repeat to yourself the word 'release' and as you repeat it let go physically any tension that you can feel in your body.

If you become aware of tension and you don't know how to release it, simply give your body a positive instruction such as 'shoulders release', 'neck release'. Don't be tempted to use negative words such as 'stop tensing up' because the subconscious mind still hears 'tensing' and responds by tightening up.

As you let go physically, you can progress to letting go of any other aspects of yourself or your life that you wish to release, such as unhealthy habits or anything that you perceive as holding you back.

When you are ready to stop, become aware of where you are now and allow yourself to feel the weight of your body on the surface that it is resting on.

Dealing with change

This book is all about making changes. You may love change or hate it, embrace it or shun it!

How do you feel about change?

You have probably developed a pattern of coping with change. Some ways of coping are to:
- thrive on it and welcome it
- pretend it's not happening
- insist that the old way is better
- accept it once you've been persuaded
- immediately accept it because it's new
- initiate change yourself

The Kübler-Ross Change Curve

Elisabeth Kübler-Ross developed the approach that follows. Life for most people has ups and downs. Most of us go through stages in response to change both personally, e.g. bereavement, redundancy, re-organisation, or general changes such as technology changing – podcasting, video-emails, new operating systems.

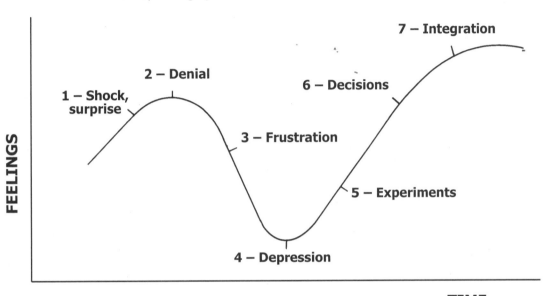

Stage 1

Shock and surprise in response to the event or change. 'I can't believe it!' – whether it's a difficult situation or a lottery win.

Stage 2

Denial of the change and finding ways to prove that it isn't happening. Sticking your head in the sand and reassuring yourself that it isn't really happening. 'I've always done it this way – these new ideas will blow over.'

Stage 3

On the way down, and experiencing anger and frustration. Often a tendency to blame everyone else and lash out at them. Still no acceptance of the change. 'Why pick on me?'

Stage 4

Hitting rock-bottom and experiencing depression and apathy. Everything seems pointless and there is no point in doing anything. 'I'm ready to give up.' Lack of self-confidence.

Stage 5

Stage 4 is so depressing that most of us start to pull ourselves out of it. This is where you will start to try out new things. 'I think I'll have a go at this – after all, anything's better than Stage 4!'

Stage 6

Deciding what works and what doesn't work. Accepting the change and beginning to feel more optimistic and enthusiastic. 'This isn't so bad after all – it actually seems to be working!'

Stage 7

At this stage, you will be integrating the change into your life so it becomes part of your norm – 'The new me!'

YOUR TRACK RECORD WITH CHANGE

Take a look to see if any of your patterns fit with the Kübler-Ross change curve. Think of situations where you have had to deal with change, and assess your track record. These could be at home, at work or any other outside-home involvement, such as voluntary work, clubs or societies.

Changes over which I had no control:

Changes I initiated:

Thinking about the situations when dealing with change:
- *things I do well are:*

- *things I could improve are:*

Over the next day or two, talk to someone who knows you well and ask them: 'In your opinion, how do I cope with change?' Jot down their reply here:

How does their view compare with how you see yourself? Is there a difference between changes at work and changes at home? Perhaps others see that you cope better than you think you do? What can you learn from the feedback that you've received?

If you are a person who thinks more about the past, it is likely that you will get stuck in feeling depressed (Stage 4) and may tend to slip back to the denial stage (Stage 2). If you are more forward-looking you may be always trying out new ideas (Stage 5) without ever actually moving on to integrate them (Stage 7). Most people have difficulty between the 5th, 6th and 7th Stages.

When Sarah was promoted to Team Leader she went on doing everything she always used to do, on top of her new responsibilities (Stage 2). She ended up very overworked and not initially recognising that she needed to allocate more work to her team. She firstly became frustrated (Stage 3) and then quite depressed (Stage 4) before realising that she would need to do things a bit differently (Stage 5). Once she began experimenting, she found the best ways to behave in her new situation. She delegated some of her most familiar tasks, and taught herself how to monitor progress (Stage 6). Once she made her new systems her own, she was fine again (Stage 7).

Your objectives

You may be clear that you want to progress in your life and work, or you may want to get more out of what you're doing now. You may simply want to take three months to review and revise your priorities in life. Whatever your objectives, make sure they're your own, and not what you think your partner, your manager, your parents, your organisation or we would want you to write.

Consider these questions before stating your overall objective. Do you:
- have any specific work or personal goals?
- want to change or get a job?
- want more time to do the things that you want to do?
- know what you want to do?
- have an overall sense of direction?
- know what you don't want to do?
- want to improve your relationships at work and/or at home?
- want to change anything about yourself? If so, what?

What are your objectives in working with this workbook (and the Springboard Women's Development Programme)?

The luck challenge

When we ask women on courses how they've achieved things in their lives, they often say: 'I was lucky' or 'It was just luck really'.

We believe that this is mostly rubbish! When we ask for anecdotal evidence, we then hear wonderful and inspiring stories of women who:

- set themselves goals or took small steps in a direction
- plucked up courage
- picked brains
- kept going despite many difficulties
- made contacts
- volunteered
- told people what they wanted
- had a positive attitude to change

They had developed the right attitude, and taken the right steps to place themselves in the right place at the right time. There was usually an opportunity open to them which they had the courage to grab, and that is the true scale of the 'Luck' that people refer to. When opportunities are there the women who use them are seen as successful. The truly determined don't even wait for opportunities, but stride out positively to make their own.

Most of us say 'it was luck' because it might seem big-headed to say:

'I was the best for the job.'

'I get on well with people.'

'I was determined to make the grade.'

'I did my background research very thoroughly.'

It feels more comfortable to say 'I was lucky!' The trouble is that after a while you start believing in lucky breaks and waiting for them to happen. You could wait for ever.

We challenge you to take any achievement which you put down to luck, and will guarantee that luck played a very small part indeed. Your luck was your own effort, determination, skills and experience.

We're not saying that there's no such thing as luck, we're simply suggesting that it has a much smaller part to play than most people credit, and that to a large extent you can make your own luck. We subscribe to this well known definition of luck:

 Luck happens when preparation meets opportunity.

This means that you have to do the preparation before you can seize the opportunity! You will, of course, have done this many times in your life already, but from now on be more aware of the amount of control you have over events.

How is the timing for you?

How are you feeling about all this now?

- impatient to get started?
- wishing you'd never decided to do this?
- anxious or eager?
- ready to make changes?

The timing will never be perfect. A good time is when you feel almost ready for change. You then need a bit of courage to take the plunge.

If you wait until you are certain, it may well be too late.

 I am trying to be myself more and more. The more confidence you have in yourself, which only comes with age and experience, the more I realise that this is you and life isn't long. So get on with it!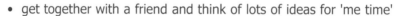

Kylie Minogue

Summary and action

In this chapter you've found out about this workbook and its approach. You've got yourself organised and you've made a start.

Action

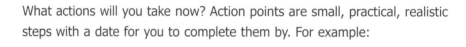

What actions will you take now? Action points are small, practical, realistic steps with a date for you to complete them by. For example:

- get together with a friend and think of lots of ideas for 'me time'
- clear a corner at home to become your workspace for using this book
- talk to your family about the support you want while you're doing this
- give yourself a treat – you've started!

Write yours here:

Specific Action **By When?**

Profile   *Rachel Bristow*

Job Title: Learning and Development Manager
Organisation: Sandwell Mental Health NHS and
Social Care Trust

I was a shy and timid child who wouldn't say 'boo
to a goose'. I still have moments where I don't feel
confident or assertive – although my family would say otherwise!

During my early school years I was bullied and found it difficult to make
friends. I hated school and couldn't wait to leave. I left school with one 'O'
level and a handful of CSEs. I was willing to work anywhere and had a series
of catering and retail jobs.

At 17 I was diagnosed with endometriosis and over the years I've had
numerous operations and hormone treatments. Although I still suffer with
this and PMS, I no longer take conventional drugs and find complementary
therapies really help with some of the symptoms.

I married when I was 19 against the advice of everyone I knew. As the
relationship grew more physically and mentally abusive, I became very
scared and anxious. Eventually I found the courage to leave and moved back
home to my parents.

My family, but particularly my parents were hugely supportive. My Dad said
they would support me as long as I undertook a qualification to get a career.
The result was a two year secretarial course. This was for me and to show
my parents I could achieve something so I worked really hard. This boosted
my confidence and I thoroughly enjoyed the experience of learning whilst
making new friends.

In 1992 I found a secretarial role within the NHS working for the School of
Nursing. At first it was daunting as I doubted my ability but my colleagues
were really supportive. That same year my dear Mum was diagnosed with a
brain tumour. I was devastated but she remained brave throughout. She

steadily improved but required a further operation that robbed her of part of her sight and gave rise to a number of problems which took away her independence. It broke my heart that life could be so unfair to such a lovely, kind person.

After a couple of secretarial moves and upgrades within the NHS, I studied for the AMSPAR qualification (The Association of Medical Secretaries, Practice Managers, Administrators and Receptionists) and remarried in 1995. I then got a job as Secretary to the Director of Personnel but never felt any satisfaction in this role.

In 1999 I gained a new manager who launched the Springboard Women's Development Programme for which I was both administrator and a participant. I realised I was capable of more and wanted more out of life. The opportunities were there if I wanted them but I hadn't had the confidence to ask for more responsibility.

I volunteered for some project work and delivered a small slot on a secretarial course. It really gave me a buzz witnessing the personal development of other people. I also attended meetings on behalf of my manager and at the same time I completed the Certificate in Personnel Practice. My boss asked me to return to subsequent Springboard programmes as a helper and then as a speaker. I was terrified but I did it!

In 2003 my world turned upside down when my Mum passed away. Her health had been deteriorating for some time but it was still a huge shock. She was my best friend and is my main inspiration in life.

In 2004 I was appointed in an HR Advisor role at Sandwell Mental Health NHS and Social Care Trust. Not long after, I had the opportunity to 'act up'. This made me step out of my comfort zone and do all sorts of things I never imagined. I was also encouraged to study for the Chartered Institute of Personnel and Development Award.

In 2005 I was appointed as a Learning and Development Manager and in September 2006 graduated with a Postgraduate Diploma in Human Resources

Development. The two years of study were hard but I could not have achieved this without the support of my husband who has been fantastic!

At 38 I finally feel happy with my achievements. It may have been a slow journey but what counts is I've got where I want to be. Who knows what the future may hold?

Learnings

- get out when the situation is no good
- have courage to make difficult decisions which you know are 'right'
- ask for more responsibility
- grasp every opportunity that comes your way

2

> *Women now have it within their power not simply to move forward as individuals, but to bring to government, business and industry a set of experiences and perspectives totally different from those which at present control them.*

Dr. Rosalind Miles – *Women and Power*

The World You Live In

Objectives
- to look at the world you live in and identify what impacts on you
- to discover what you know and don't know about the world around you
- to see the bigger picture so that you can decide later what is important for you and your future

This chapter is important because

- you may feel powerful or powerless to influence the world you live in
- the world is changing so quickly and you need to know what affects you in your work and personal life

Contents
- your personal power and influence
- your power net
- big global issues versus small local issues
- facts of the world you live in
- women's lives in the UK
- trends in organisations
- how people get recognition
- summary and action
- profile of Elisabeth Winkler

The world that you live in begins with the people you live with and if you live alone it begins at your doorstep. It also arrives in your home through television, the internet, radio and telephone or mobile if you have all or any of these. From the moment we write this and you read it the world you live in changes every second.

You may be very interested and informed about the world that you live in, too busy surviving in it to look any further than the immediate things around you, ignorant about it, naïve, cynical or have a healthy scepticism about it.

Depending on your age, you may be able to see how amazingly the world has changed in your life time or how it has changed from your mother's or your grandmother's generation (even if you were not brought up with them). She (or you), perhaps, could not have imagined a generation or so ago someone in the UK talking directly on a mobile phone to someone in Australia and then sending a photograph or a short video of the scene she (or you) are looking at.

Not only is the world changing at a dramatic and accelerating rate but also information about these changes is more readily available through the media and the Internet. When you plan your future or make decisions about your life, you have available to you today masses more information than your grandmother did when she was your age. If you can access it and filter it for relevance, this information about the world and what is happening in it can help you make more informed choices.

For some women, however, there is so much information available that it puts them off looking. This deluge of information can seem daunting and the thought of influencing the world can simply feel too big. In this chapter we will highlight a few current facts to stimulate thought, stir up feelings and motivate you into action and throughout the rest of the book there will be a few more facts to keep you thinking.

Taking a fresh look at the world about you may give you the clues you need about what you want to do with your life, or may highlight things that you feel energised to do something about. You can decide how to view the reality of the world you live in either from a positive perspective:

The world for women is so much better these days and I can influence making it even better in small and possibly huge ways.

or from a negative perspective:

Isn't it awful all the horrible things that are happening still for women and I can't do anything about it?

or, of course from anywhere in between.

So, first of all, let's look at your power and influence. We believe that women have much more power and influence than they may realise.

Your personal power and influence

You do not operate in a vacuum. The opportunities that are open to you, the way you are perceived, your ability to influence people, your ability to make things happen, the chances of having your own values met, are all influenced by your confidence in yourself, your judgement and your abilities as well as the culture of your organisation and/or the community you live in. Some women feel that as individuals they have very little power, either in their community or the organisation in which they work.

Organisational culture, and the use of influence inside organisations, is often assumed to be about playing office politics, playing games, or becoming another rat in the rat race but it could simply be about understanding what goes on and about being strategic in the way you influence others.

Your personal power is your ability to influence others

At work, at home and in your community, you may have more ability to influence what's going on around you than you think! If you ask someone to do something, and they do it, then clearly you had the ability to influence that person – you were using your personal power in that situation.

Organisational culture and the use of power are entirely neutral. They are the oil that lubricates the cogs of the organisation and the organisation could, of course, be your family, community or social network.

Your power and influence takes several forms.

Formal authority

This is the power invested in you by your job title or your role e.g. shift leader, mother. Anyone doing your job/role would have your formal authority. It manifests itself in the right to make decisions, and the right to insist that someone does something.

Expertise

This is the power given to you by your specialist knowledge, skills, experience and qualifications. The more exclusive the expertise and the more useful in your social group or workplace, the more power and influence it gives you.

Resource control

Someone may do what you ask them to do because you control their access to something that they want. This power is the control of physical, financial or informational resources. For example: allocation of car parking spaces, issuing pocket money, access to people, being Treasurer of the playgroup, whether you tell everything that happened at the union meeting, etc. People in relatively lowly hierarchical positions often have a great deal of resource control power, but the most valued resources are usually money and information.

Interpersonal skills

This is the power you have in the way you get on with people, your ability to persuade and to build good quality relationships, your assertiveness. This is the most potent form of power and one that women are said to be good at.

Your power questionnaire

The following questionnaire is designed to help you think about the power you have, and although it was designed for people in paid employment, the same factors have influence in a voluntary group, family or community:

Formal authority

Do you have the formal right (say, in your job description or role) to make decisions, other than trivial ones?

Do other people need your approval before they take action?

Do you supervise someone else's work?

Do your decisions significantly affect important aspects of your group or department's work long-term?

Does your manager/partner typically support your decisions and not overrule them?

Do you encounter any resistance to your right to make decisions, supervise others, and give approval, from subordinates, peers, and more senior people? (If you do, this suggests a reduction in your power which you may need to do something about).

Expertise

Does it take a year or longer to learn to do your job or role adequately?

Do you need a qualification to do your job/role?

What is the highest qualification in your field? Do you have it?

Are you the only person who can do your job/role?

If you were to leave, would they have difficulty replacing you?

Does your knowledge and skill relate to a major aspect of the group or department's work?

Do people frequently consult you and follow your advice?

Do more senior people clearly show that they value your contribution?

Resource control

Can you give or withhold access to the following resources?
- money
- information
- ideas
- training
- other people
- computers or internet access
- perks
- time

Add any others that you control:

Interpersonal skills

Do you make sure that other people take your views seriously when it matters to you?

Are you on good terms with a number of people across different departments and hierarchical levels at work or family, friends and community outside of work?

Do people confide in you?

Are you good at speaking up?

Are you an active listener? Do you make sure you have understood the other person's point of view?

Do you avoid being either passive or aggressive in formal or informal discussion with others at home or work?

Can you hold the attention of a group or larger audience?

Material used, with permission, from Dr Margaret Ryan's work in *Power and Influence in Organisations,* originally published by The Training Agency.

Your Power Net

Overleaf is a diagram of your own power net. Put your own name in the bubble in the centre, as shown in the example. In the other bubbles put the names of individual people who have an important effect on your life. They may be higher or lower than you in the hierarchy at work, and either inside or outside an organisation. Use the names of individuals and not whole departments, because your power is based on individual relationships.

You may want to re-draw the diagram for your life outside of work. Add extra bubbles if you need to.

Using the four categories of power outlined on the previous page, assess which sorts of power you are using in your relationship with each person.

RACHEL'S POWER NET

1 Formal Authority
2 Expertise
3 Resource Control
4 Interpersonal Skills

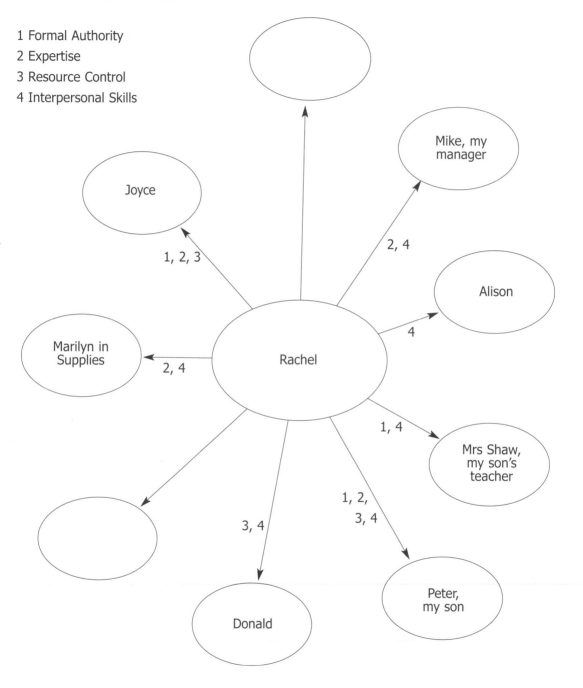

YOUR POWER NET

1 Formal Authority
2 Expertise
3 Resource Control
4 Interpersonal Skills

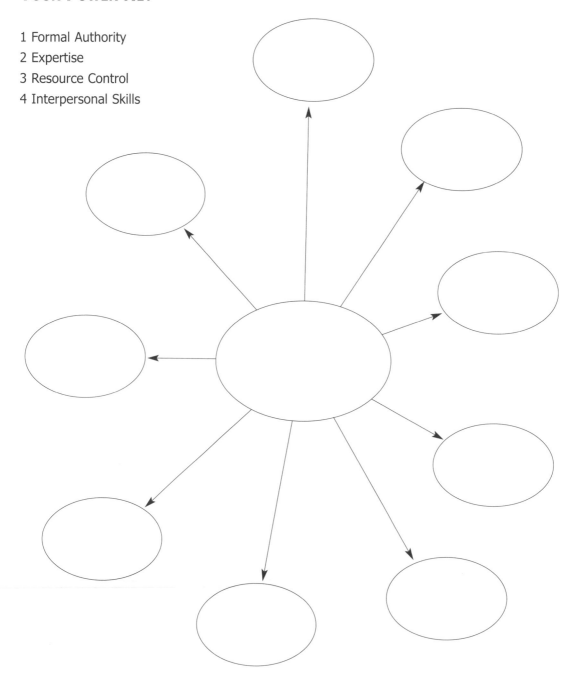

You can also do the exercise the other way round and consider what form of power people are using to influence you.

What does it mean?

What have you discovered about how you use your own power? Are you using all your sources of power and influence effectively? Many women underestimate their ability to influence things around them, so you may not have done yourself justice in this exercise. Most women's power is based on using good interpersonal skills.

Make your notes here:

What do you want to change about your power and influence?

The impression of power

Having the formal authority, expertise or resource control is not always enough. Being seen to have it is important. Other people's willingness to be influenced hinges largely on their perception of you, or the impression you create: in other words, your credibility!

At a meeting Anne may have the most expertise on a particular subject, be the most up-to-date and have the most relevant information on it. Also at the meeting is Tina who knows a great deal less about the subject, but creates the impression that she is a real expert. Tina's ability to influence the meeting may be as great, if not greater, than Anne's, because Tina has more credibility. Sadly, unless Anne does a better job on the image she creates, her group or organisation may not realise the value of her expertise until after she's left.

So don't assume that people remember your expertise, respect your formal authority, recognise your resource control and value your interpersonal skills. It's up to you to be proud of what you've got going for you and decide how and when to use it positively.

Big global issues versus small local issues

Where does one begin and the other end? Global warming and the numbers of people living at poverty levels throughout the world may seem huge and remote, while joining in the local recycling scheme or buying a copy of 'The Big Issue' from a homeless person on your local High Street may seem more within your sphere. Calculating the impact of transporting food worldwide may seem enormous and daunting, while deciding to buy locally sourced food that has not travelled far (or not to buy some or all foods from a supermarket at all) may be possible.

Think about what you already know or could easily find out.

List 10 foods that you buy regularly and then add where they come from.

Food   **Origin**

Now think about 10 people in your workplace, the street where you live, at your children's school (if you have children) or at any local group that you belong to.

Who they are?   **What is their racial background?**   **Where were they born?**

Now repeat the questions for some of your favourite sport or TV programme participants.

Who they are?   **What is their racial background?**   **Where were they born?**

Just on these two issues alone things will have changed from a generation ago. The world is increasingly global.

Which issues in your local community or the wider world do you feel strongly about?

What do you want to find out more about?

What are you going to do to become more informed or make a difference?

Global issues

Which issues interest you? Do you prefer to hear the good news i.e.

- a new safe playground on an old housing estate?
- the saving of thousands of people in a recent disaster?
- work that is happening to solve the challenge of cancer?
- the joy that a group of disabled people has when they hear that they have been given a Lottery grant to build a new day centre?

Or do you have concerns about:

- the environment such as global warming or pollution?
- activities for young people in your local community that help reduce crime or drug abuse?
- the plight of women in other countries where their births are not recognised or they are not allowed to leave their homes or be seen by anyone but their family?
- the pros and cons of a local road project?
- the health and welfare of street children in Brazil or India?
- the growth in drug traffic and the way it could end up affecting young people that you know?

Or do you not think about anything like this?

Most people are touched in some way by what is going on around them and can do something about it too.

There is increasing evidence of a new determination amongst women who are not inclined to accept the lives that others decide for them and want to take more control over their own lives.

> *No longer are women an 'other' knocking at the door to be let into society. Women now have gone beyond this point, reaching a stage where they no longer want to integrate themselves into men's world so much as to reshape the world, make it something better.*

Shere Hite

Don't underestimate your influence

Often people feel very strongly about an issue but also feel totally unable to do anything about it. Keep your eyes and ears open for examples of individual people living ordinary lives, changing big things, little by little, by standing up to be counted, and by acting locally. The influence of local initiatives such as road safety campaigns, rape crisis centres and recycling projects can be inspiring examples of the difference each of us can make – you just need to start!

One woman, who had never left the UK before, presented and won her case in the European Court. This resulted in changes in the laws about the use of noxious chemicals, as her son had died due to the lack of control over the chemicals used in the garage where he worked.

Never doubt that a small group of committed citizens can change the world, indeed it is the only thing that ever has. ,

Margaret Mead

Facts of the world you live in

Browse through these facts, think about how familiar you are with them and where you spot new or surprising information.

Population

In the last 30 years the population of Britain has grown from less than 55 million to 58 million. There are now 1 million more men and 0.6 million more women aged 65 or over than in the 1970s. There are 24 million households in Britain, and 7 million families with dependent children. These include 5.2 million families headed by couples, 1.6 million headed by a lone mother and 180,000 headed by a lone father.

Sources: ONS (2005) Population Trends Winter 2005; ONS (2005) Focus on Families

Age group	Females		Males	
	thousands	*%*	*thousands*	*%*
Under 16	5,489	18	5,773	20
16 – 64	18,847	63	18,668	66
65 and over	5,353	18	3,994	14
All ages	29,690	100	28,435	100

Source: ONS (2005) Mid-2004 population estimates, corrected December 2005

The population also includes an estimated:

10 million disabled people [1]

4.6 million people from ethnic minorities

3.1 million belonging to a non-Christian religion

2.3 – 3.2 million gay, lesbian or bisexual adults

1. Reporting a limiting long-term illness or disability that restricts daily activities.

Sources: ONS (2004) Census 2001 National report for England and Wales; GROS (2004)

Scotland's Census 2001; DTI (2004) Final regulatory impact assessment: Civil Partnership Act

2004

Women's lives in the UK

Since 1975 women's employment has increased from around 6 out of 10 to 7 out of 10 (70%) for women of working age (16 – 59): men's employment has declined from around 9 out of 10 to 8 out of 10 (79%) for men of working age (16 – 64).

Source: ONS (2005) Labour Market Statistics – Time Series Data

Overall, women's earnings are 82% of men's...

Source: "Pay and Income", Women and Equality Unit (www.womenandequalityunit.gov.uk)

In 2003, just 3.7% of FTSE 100 executive directors were women...

Source: "Are we there yet?"

Women made up 20% of MPs in 2005... The number of Black and Minority Ethnic women MPs is still very unrepresentative, standing at just 0.3%... There have only ever been 3 Black women MPs.

Source: "30 years of closing the gap between men and women", Fawcett Society, November 2005

One third of FTSE 100 companies still have a men-only board.

Source: "Money Money Money: Is it still a rich man's world? An audit of women's economic welfare in Britain", Fawcett Society, March 2005

Part-time and flexible working

Employees aged 16 – 64 in Great Britain:

	Women		Men	
	thousands	*%*	*thousands*	*%*
Part-time	4,845	42	1,093	9
Flexitime	1,387	12	1,055	9
Annualised hours	514	4	524	4
Term-time working	888	8	162	1
Job share	150	1	16	*
Homeworking [1]	195	2	124	1
Any flexible arrangement	6,538	57	2,766	23

1. Working in own home or in same grounds/building

* Less than 0.5%

NB Employees with more than one flexible arrangement are included in each figure, but only once in the total

Source: ONS (2005) Labour Force Survey Spring 2005 dataset

Public and political life

Women's representation in the UK Parliament has increased from 27 women elected in October 1974, to 126 women MPs in 2006 (an increase from 4.3% to 19.5%). This contrasts markedly with the Scottish Parliament (40% women) and the National Assembly for Wales (50% women), where more equal representation has been achieved through positive action by some political parties.

Sources: House of Commons Information Office (2004) Women in the House of Commons; UK Parliament (2006) Members of Parliament by gender: numbers, updated 10/2/06; The Scottish Parliament (2005) Female MSPs: Session 2; National Assembly for Wales (2005) Who? – Elected members

Overall the political parties were represented as follows in 2006:

Political party	Women		Men	
	Number of MPs	% of party	Number of MPs	% of party
Conservative	17	9	179	91
Labour	96	27	257	73
Liberal Democrats	9	14	54	86
Other parties [1]	4	12	30	88
All parties	126	20	520	80

1. Includes Speaker & deputies

Source: UK Parliament (2006) Members of Parliament by gender: numbers, updated 10 February 2006

There are only 2 ethnic minority women MPs at Westminster, and 13 men. All 4 Muslim MPs are men.

Source: BBC (2005) Record number of new minority MPs, 10 May 2005

Asian women make up less than 1% of local councillors in England, and there are no Muslim women who are MPs

Source: Women and Work Commission Report "Shaping a Fairer Future", February 2006

Women make up only 29% of councillors in England, compared to 52% of the adult population (aged 21 and over).

Source: Women and Work Commission Report "Shaping a Fairer Future", February 2006

An annual set of indicators of women's representation in a range of areas shows, for example:

- around 3 in 10 head teachers in secondary schools and FE college principals are women, compared with only 1 in 9 university vice chancellors
- a quarter of Civil Service top management are women
- only 10% of senior police officers and 9% of the senior judiciary are women
- less than 1% of senior ranks in the armed forces are women

Source: EOC (2006) Sex and power: who runs Britain? 2006

81% of administrative and secretarial employees are women.

Source: "Facts about Women and Men in Great Britain 2006", Equal Opportunity Commission

... women make up only 32% of managers and senior officials.

Source: "A fair deal for women in the workplace", Women and Work Commission, March 2005

Domestic violence is the second most reported crime, accounting for about 25% of violent incidents reported to the police.

Source: www.bullyonline.org.uk

Only 5.3% of reported rapes end in a conviction.

Source: "Rape victims 'failed by police and courts'", The Independent, 31 January 2007

Just think about how these facts would have been different 10, 20, 30 years ago?

Trends in organisations

E-mail, the Internet, intranet and mobile phones are now commonplace.

The concept of a career or job for life is totally obsolete.

Public sector organisations have become more entrepreneurial and income-generating.

Organisations are reducing the numbers of full time employees and instead are contracting out work to freelance people and/or increasing the numbers of part-time employees.

The 'Opportunity Now' campaign has raised awareness of women's career issues in hundreds of organisations.

Mainstream organisations are now treating global warming and green issues seriously.

Flexible working patterns such as job-sharing, term-time only working and flexitime and other family-friendly policies are on the increase.

Greater contribution to the 'bottom line' is being required from individual departments, units and managers.

Women and older workers represent under-developed sources of labour for employers.

Spot recent initiatives in your organisation, such as:

- more internet trading
- involvement in NVQs (National Vocational Qualifications)
- gaining or keeping Investors In People
- support for Open University courses
- women-only courses
- career breaks and flexi-working
- corporate social responsibility projects

Add any others:

Take a look at your own organisation

In a huge and diverse organisation some of the general culture may affect you greatly, or have only a small effect. In a small organisation it may affect every aspect of your work. It's likely that the day-to-day culture of your own workplace has a dramatic effect on your morale, and your opportunities for change.

THINK THROUGH THESE ASPECTS

What is the structure of your organisation?

Are there particular areas where people get promoted quickly? If so – which?

What is highly valued, e.g. loyalty, bright ideas, independence of thought, long service, attention to detail?

What is the general attitude to people outside your workplace?

Which people hold the influence, e.g. people who make the boss laugh, people who have been there a long time?

Is there an inner circle of people who hold the influence? If so – why? How can an outsider get to know them?

What are the anecdotes that are told fondly about the organisation or about past members of the organisation?

Where is the organisation going? Is there a sense of direction?

What do you know about the people who use your organisation's goods/services?

Who decides what happens in your workplace?

Overall, how is the culture of your own place of work affecting you and your ability to achieve your ambitions?

WHAT DOES IT ALL MEAN TO YOU?

Considering all these facts and trends:

What surprises you or confirms what you already know?

What opportunities are offered to you by these facts and trends?

What threats are posed to you by these facts and trends?

How will they influence the important people in your work life?

How will they influence the important people in your personal life?

How people get recognition

If you're waiting to get promoted, move sideways, or change your job in any way, it is important to work out a further aspect of how things happen in organisations.

Research by Harvey Coleman (ex-IBM) across a number of large organisations identified three factors that determine whether someone is promoted or not:

Performance

the reality of how good your work actually is.

Image

the impression you create about yourself and your work. Some people are overlooked for promotion because while their work is actually good they give the impression of being confused, negative, unable to cope, or not interested in promotion.

Visibility

whether people know of you and how well you work. This means raising your profile, becoming more visible and building your contacts. You may do a great job, have a great image, but if the right people don't know that you exist – you won't get promoted or get the recognition for the work that you do.

The contribution of each of these factors to people being promoted were:

It may seem outrageous that the quality of your work contributes only 10% towards getting you promotion or recognition, but if you're in an organisation where everyone does a good job the other two factors assume greater and greater significance.

There are usually several people who are capable of doing the job – the person who gets it also has her image and visibility working for her. These statistics are not saying 'Don't bother to do a good job' but they are saying:

'Do a good job, but don't think anyone's going to promote you for it!'

'Do a good job, but put some effort into building your image, and increasing your visibility as well.'

These statistics go a long way towards explaining 'The Flossie Trap'.

The Flossie trap

There is no significance in calling this particular trap after 'Flossie', so our apologies to anyone called Florence or Flossie, but it is a phenomenon which affects women much more than men.

There is usually a Flossie in every organisation, and often one in every family or community. There may be several.

Flossie is the person who thinks that promotion or recognition comes with doing a good job. She believes that if she works well enough and hard enough, someone will notice and reward her. If promotion doesn't come along, she may interpret that as implying she's not working well enough, so she works even harder and better.

Flossie is holding the place together.

Flossie may never be promoted, because the whole place or project would fall apart – it's much better to take the risk with someone who's not indispensable.

Flossie is indispensable. Flossie is often asked to train up new people who then get promoted over her head.

At home Flossie believes that people do appreciate her – it's just that they're too busy to show it.

As Flossie doesn't know that 90% of the reason whether she gets promotion or recognition or not is due to her image and visibility, she doesn't make any efforts to improve her interpersonal skills and her appearance, and she regards building contacts as a waste of time.

Flossie can end up bitter, frustrated, exhausted and STUCK.

YOUR FLOSSIE RATING

When have you been a Flossie (many women have!) and are you still one now in some areas of your life?

What do you want to do about it?

Summary and action

In this chapter you've looked at just some of the things that are going on around you and begun to assess where the opportunities lie for a change.

Further optional reading

Charles Handy – *Beyond Certainty* – published by Arrow Books
Robin Norwood – *Women who love too much* – published by Arrow Books
Dale Spender – *Nattering on the Net* – published by Spinifex

Action

What action are you going to take to make the most of the opportunities open to you?

Here are some suggestions:

- find out about any open learning facilities in my organisation or area
- find out more about being self-employed or going on contract
- build up my contacts in other parts of the organisation
- join a network that relates to things I want to change
- decide whether I'm happy being a Flossie or not
- speak out about how I feel about cruelty to animals
- refer to Chapter 14 for other books to read, websites to visit

Write yours here:

Specific Action   **By When?**

Profile *Elisabeth Winkler*

Job Title: Editor
Organisation: Living Earth, Soil Association Magazine

I was a lost 1970's London teenager. I refused my
university place, and became a voluntary helper in a
therapeutic community treating mental illness without
drugs. It was experimental, like a boot camp for the emotions – and
I include it in my CV. Three years later, aged 21, I was on a new mission:
rescuing my heroin addict boyfriend. Then came pregnancy; knowing from
the community about the importance of a child's early experiences, I faced up
to a hard truth – I had to forsake my destructive relationship with the father
of my child.

After seeing a poster in a wholefood shop about natural childbirth, I turned
up at the Birth Centre where I was asked for my help answering the office's
helpline. That (unpaid) job put me on track for the rest of my career. I learnt
about giving accurate information, as well as lobbying and reporting. I then
trained with the National Childbirth Trust to teach women and their partners
coping skills for labour. The strengthening practices I taught (controlled
breathing and yoga postures to relax and assist nature) became life skills for
my own health. I also co-founded a voluntary group, which set up a birthing
room in our local Bath hospital.

By this time, 1982, I was living in Somerset with a beautiful man, twice my age
and a writer. We'd met by chance when my daughter was a baby. With him I
had two more daughters, and worked on my writing. But I needed money.
I approached *Parents* magazine thinking I'd have to tone down my alternative
approach but this was just what the editor wanted. From 1985 she showered
me with commissions and my husband editor ruthlessly cut and rearranged
my copy to make it flow. I was in awe of his talent but in time, as he had
promised, I acquired those skills myself.

My husband died at home in 1986. I found it hard to grieve. I threw myself
into turning out polished pieces and also contributed to the Sunday Times

Magazine. In 1988 I had a chance encounter that yielded both a lifetime friend and a dear colleague. Working freelance is isolating and this dear friend has given me a sense of my own worth. We all need believing mirrors to reflect back that we can do it.

My youngest daughter was diagnosed with learning difficulties – another rewarding challenge. I remarried and moved to Bristol with my three girls to live with my new husband. A chance chat with a fellow school mother led me to help her expose the inadequate cardiac surgical record at Bristol Royal Infirmary, a campaign that laid the foundation for a public enquiry in 1998. I also did video interviewing of Holocaust survivors for the Spielberg archive. Both roles (enlightening yet mostly unpaid) sprung from my belief that acknowledging suffering is vital to healing.

As well as writing for the national women's glossy magazines and the broadsheets, I had a political column in the Bristol Evening Post – at last I could air my own (people before profit) views. But working freelance was uncertain: I needed a salary. In 2001, aged 47 and now divorced, I became magazine editor for the Soil Association, the organic food charity. I heard about the job through a chance contact – I might not otherwise have had the courage to apply. Now I am on the payroll working for a cause close to my heart. Like the National Childbirth Trust, the Soil Association is another post-war charity, founded to resist mindless industrialisation (in this case of farming) and restore respect for nature.

Working for causes I believe in, is, I realise, vital for my wellbeing. I met my partner at a music festival – both in our early 50s, we love drumming and dancing. Now, as well as developing my freelance work, we are co-creating a website **www.pearl-barley.com** where people can share ideas about a green sustainable future.

Learnings

- charities are great sources of professional training
- volunteering, if you can afford it, is another great training
- listen to your gut instinct
- life is the best teacher and shows you parts of yourself you never knew existed!

3

> *I want to stop being my own worst enemy and start being my best friend. I want to decide who I am, mostly, and what work I want to do, seriously.*

Judy Simmons

Who Are You?

Objectives
- to assess who you are now
- to make the most of the best of you

This chapter is important because

- understanding who you are and what you believe in helps you take the next step
- learning from your experiences moves you onwards
- identifying your values clarifies your goals
- letting go of old patterns helps you think more freely about the future

Contents
- your whole self
- overcoming prejudice
- becoming an experiencing person
- your values
- your attitude
- summary and action
- profile of Gaye Mallows

Knowing yourself

Whoever you are and wherever you are in your life you have this workbook because you are a woman wanting to change something or do things better or differently in the future.

The UK has legislation making it illegal to discriminate against a person on account of gender, race, colour, disability, age, sexuality, and religion. Organisations declare themselves as 'Equal Opportunities' or 'Diversity' employers. The past climate however, has resulted in the majority of senior posts being held by **men** and **white, heterosexual, non-disabled people**.

Your whole self

If you are white, heterosexual and able-bodied, it may be that you have not thought much about some of the issues that follow. On the other hand you may have thought a great deal about them because they are very relevant to you or to someone close to you. Work through all the parts of the chapter so that you take in issues for other women as well as for yourself.

In our society there is considerable prejudice and discrimination against minority groups. Prejudice is the prejudgement of a person, not based on reason or knowledge. Prejudice affects the behaviour of both the minority and the majority. Prejudice usually arises out of fear and lack of knowledge. Acting on our prejudices can lead to discrimination. Often women have experienced discrimination but pass it off as 'humour' or worse don't recognise it.

Being a woman

Being a woman is at the core of who you are. Usually the first thing that people notice about each other is the gender that they are. Some people have changed their gender, usually after a long process. So if you have had your gender re-assigned you will have thought a lot about what it means to you to be a woman. Otherwise being a woman is all you have known and you may or may not have thought about it very much. Your relationship to your gender may also be hugely affected by surgery (mastectomy, hysterectomy), inability/difficulty in conceiving or by the menopause.

Being your age now

At the age that you are now you are likely to have experiences in common with other people around the same age. Although some of these may reflect patterns general to women and men from earlier generations, their experiences will have been substantially different. At your age in the 21st century, communications around the world, access to information, morality and standards of behaviour, and many more aspects of life are very different from how they were in your mother's or grandmother's day. Similarly how you experienced life 10 or 20 years ago is very different from how people 10 or 20 years younger than you are experiencing life now.

Ever thought how it would be
if I were You or You were Me
and what exactly we might see,
hear, touch, taste, smell and feel if
I were You or You were Me?
WONDERFUL THING DIVERSITY!

Sue Bearder

Being your race or ethnic origin

Similarly, being the race that you are may open or close doors for you. An International Millennium Survey showed that in Britain 92% of people believe that racism is commonplace, higher than any other country. An EOC study 'Moving on Up' published in 2007 found that Pakistani, Bangladeshi and black Caribbean women find it harder to get jobs and win promotion despite good qualifications.

A Commission for Racial Equality report, "Employment and Ethnicity", published in 2005, showed the differences in hourly pay rates for men and women from different ethnic groups.

Black and minority ethnic women are 3 times more likely to be unemployed than white women.

Source: Women & Equality Unit, quoting figures taken from Labour Force Survey, Spring 2004

'
When I was a child, it did not occur to me, even once, that the black in which I was encased (I called it brown in those days) would be considered one day beautiful. Considered beautiful and called beautiful by great groups.
'

Gwendolyn Brooks

Being with or without an impairment

Impairment is the loss of a physical, sensory or mental function or loss or partial loss of one or more organs or limbs, visible or hidden. It may mean having a severe impairment or having a minor impairment, such as being short sighted, which may stop you getting some jobs. Being physically different in any way affects the way people are treated. Disability is the loss or limitation of opportunity to take an equal part in society.

Having your spiritual or religious beliefs

The UK is now a multi-faith country and many people follow specific, clear and defined spiritual or religious paths, while others have no belief in such matters at all. Your spiritual beliefs or lack of them may be a large or small part in your life.

Being the sexuality that you are

This means being heterosexual, lesbian, bisexual or transsexual. Your sexuality may not play a huge part in your life and your arrival at your current sense of who you are sexually may be something that you have given little thought to. Or it may have been a long and challenging process for you to be who you are now with your sexuality.

Overcoming prejudice

Your sex, sexuality, age, race, colour and level of impairment may all have an impact on the people you meet. The degree of impact varies according to the degree of prejudice you hold and meet. When prejudice continues over a period of time, people change their behaviour to overcome it, fight it or give in to it. You may experience prejudice from others or you may be prejudiced about others.

To overcome yours or other people's prejudice, what parts of your behaviour do you want to change if you encounter prejudice on account of:	People being prejudiced about me	My prejudice about other people
Being a woman?		
Your age?		
Your race or colour?		
Your level of physical ability or impairment?		
Your spirituality/religion?		
Your sexuality?		
Anything unusual about you? e.g. class, being very tall/short		

Becoming an experiencing person

Becoming a fully experiencing person means:

- learning from your experience
- being open to what life brings you
- having a positive attitude to life
- regarding failure as an opportunity to learn and grow
- actively changing and growing
- learning something new from every year of your life, rather than experiencing the same year over and over again
- meeting every new situation afresh without old preconceptions or rules affecting you
- being an independent thinker; thinking things out for yourself instead of accepting other people's views
- having a healthy curiosity about your past and what you can learn from it to help you in the future

The following exercise exploits your healthy curiosity and extends your process of learning from everything that has happened to you.

THIS IS YOUR LIFE

List the events that have happened in your life so far. Events can be:

- something you remember for no specific reason
- happy or sad
- fearful, funny or embarrassing
- success or failure
- challenging
- new or repetitious
- very short experiences, anything from a chance remark that sticks in your head, to a summer holiday
- life changing or insignificant

People usually remember more if they start now and go backwards, so start with your age now and work backwards, just putting a key word or two for each event until you reach your earliest memory. Do it briskly without going into too much detail. If you want more room transfer this on to a bigger sheet of paper.

MY LIFE

Now show pictorially on this page how your life has been. Be as creative as you like with how you show it.

You can draw a graph of the ups and downs, draw pictures, take a larger sheet and cut out pictures from magazines to represent the events. Use colour and shapes if you wish.

We live our lives forwards but we can only understand them backwards.

Søren Kierkegaard

Tracking the Themes Down

Look at the picture or graph as if it were someone else's and pick out the themes. Timing is a theme and a good place to start.

What major events have you experienced earlier or later than most people? e.g.

- death of a close friend or relative
- taking responsibility for others
- notable achievements
- gaining qualifications
- experiencing serious illness
- marriage/civil partnership/birth/divorce
- puberty/menopause

Have a look for other themes. What strikes you most as you look at your chart?

What themes or threads run through your life?

What are the key turning points?

What do you see that you would like to let go of? e.g. themes, relationships that are not helping you, ties that are binding you to the past, humiliations, resentments

How do you rate yourself in terms of success/failure?

What have you learnt from this exercise?

Your values

Your approach to life is based on a set of beliefs that you have acquired over the course of your life so far. Some of these will be truly yours and some may have been acquired from the environment you have lived in. All your decisions are based on what you value. Values are your beliefs, and give you the criteria by which you measure things.

Very often, when people say 'I can't...' what they really mean is 'I don't choose to...'

You are making lots of choices about your life all day, every day in the way that you:

- choose to behave
- respond or react to situations
- prioritise your time/place in relationships and activities
- spend your money
- spend your time
- relate to the rest of the world/your community
- think and feel about yourself

If you are indecisive, then even choosing not to choose also affects the way you spend your life, so there's no avoiding your own influence! The way you make these day-to-day split-second choices is strongly influenced by what matters to you and what you believe in – that is, your values. Knowing your values tells you what you want to do, don't want to do, are likely to enjoy doing or feel strongly about.

Values change over time, i.e. as you get older, and/or as circumstances change. For example, starting work, having children, being left alone. Finding new information often triggers the connection to our values. If you read a newspaper article, see a film or TV programme, find something on the Internet or hear something from a friend it is seldom that you are neutral to the information. Usually you have a response or reaction to the information. Most people have a pattern of response. Is it good news that really captures your imagination or is it the negative news that fires your feelings? Your responses could be:

Neutral – no strong feelings or apathetic, don't care, not affected

Positive – happy, pleased, energised, ecstatic, interested, moved to tears, joyful

Angry – irritated, annoyed, furious, outraged

Sad – upset, depressed, tearful

Fearful – anxious, frightened, scared, apprehensive, petrified

Guilty – ashamed, responsible, it's my fault

The type and strength of your response usually indicates that the news you have received matches or crosses one of your values.

Think back to the facts given in Chapter 2 and read the following information to see what arouses feelings in you that may be related to your values. Most of the information given shows an improvement on the situation for women 30 years ago.

There are 771 million illiterate persons in the world. Two thirds of them are women.
Source: Unesco (www.uis.unesco.org)

529,000 women die unnecessarily each year as a consequence of pregnancy and childbirth. 98% of these deaths occur in developing countries.
Source: World Health Organisation (www.who.org)

Of the world's 1.2 billion people living in poverty, 70% are women.
Source: Oxfam (www.oxfam.org)

If the world's richest countries honoured their aid commitments for just 5 years, the debt of the poorest could be written off to such a degree that the basic health and education needs of the world's poorest people could be met.
Source: New Economics Foundation report, 'Debt relief as if people mattered', June 2006

Women spent an average of 19 hours a week on chores – men only 5.5 hours.
Source: Institute for Social and Economic Research report "Housework and Paid Work: Continuing Contrasts in the Time Spent by Husbands and Wives", July 2003

In 2.41 million families – 3 out of 4 families – at least 1 parent regularly works at least 1 day every weekend, and 1 in 5 families have a parent regularly working both weekend days.
Source: National Centre for Social Research report, "Keeping time for children", 2004

Across all employees:
- 48% could work flexi-time
- 41% could job share if needed
- 20% could work from home
- 35% could take parental leave
- 24% said childcare help was available to them – an increase from only 4% since 1998.

Source: from the 2004 Second Work-life Balance Survey (Employees) carried out by Mori for the DTI

Values

Values relate to the four different areas of your life – the world/community, work, relationships and yourself. All these areas overlap, may be in conflict, and may have common denominators. For example – valuing working for the community versus wanting or needing to make a lot of money may create a dilemma.

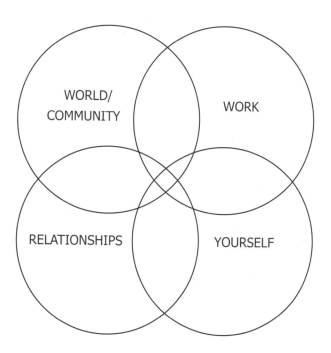

WHAT DO YOU VALUE?

What matters to YOU? What is important? What do you value?

Write down the things you value on the chart on page 61, use the examples to give you ideas – or cover them up if you wish to be left free to find your own ideas first.

At work

a job

money

challenge and interest

environmental impact

responsibility

travel

working with people

variety of tasks

producing a product/service I value

For the world/community

a safer crossing near the school

litter being cleared from the High Street

peace

no cruelty to children

everyone with food and water

free political systems

stop global warming

no cruelty to animals

In your relationships

honesty

someone special

children of my own

shared values

sense of humour

security

to be valued as me

For yourself

sense of humour

peace of mind

following a spiritual path

time to dig the garden

good health

a nice car

house decorated to my taste

having self respect

time to read a book

Value	I MUST have	I would like to have	It would be nice to have
Work			
World/ Community			
Relationships			
Myself			

Meeting values raises energy

When your values aren't being met, it gives rise to dissatisfaction, complaints and niggles, and your energy drains away.

When your values are being met, it brings satisfaction and good feeling, and your energy rises. Values are so personal that no two people have the same lists. There are no right values or wrong values, only your values.

On the chart on page 61 tick your values that are being met at the moment.

Sharing values

Some people find it easier to share personal things such as values with people they are really close to. Others prefer to share with people they don't know so well.

Sharing has the advantages that you:
• become clearer about your own ideas
• pick up hints and tips from others
• think about and assess what you've written

There is no need to get very heavy about it – even though values are a serious personal issue. Get together with, or telephone two or three other women and share your ideas. Then add any new ideas to your list.

Are you fulfilled?

If you have values in the 'I must have' section which aren't being met, then these may give you the clues about the goals that you want to set for the future.

In the 'I must have' column for the world it may seem daunting to think of tackling world hunger or pollution. Acknowledge the values now and wait till later to think about how you will meet them.

If people have large numbers of unfulfilled values in the 'I must have' section, they may respond by:

- gaining the drive and determination to do something about it
- becoming bitter and cynical
- daydreaming wistfully about what might have been
- complaining that life isn't fair

How do you feel about your fulfilled values?

How do you feel about your unfulfilled values?

Which unfulfilled values do you want to do something about?

If you were to distil your values down to seven words that you could use to check out your future decisions, what would these words be?

For me, would this be e.g. joyful, fun, peaceful, easy, exciting, challenging?

Your attitude

Your attitude to life develops out of your experiences, and the way you think and feel, and is THE KEY to your success.

Here are some examples of positive and negative attitudes which will greatly affect the outcome of situations. Some of them affect situations so dramatically that they become self-fulfilling prophecies:

Negative	Positive
Where's the catch?	Where's the opportunity?
I'm better than you	I am equal to you
This will never work	I'll make this work
I'm not worth this	I am worth this
I've heard it all before	What can I learn here?
I can't do this	I can do this
What's wrong with this?	What's right with this?
I'll make a fool of myself	I'll learn something
I'm too old	I'm not too old

Your attitude colours how people see you.

Your attitude can warm the space between you and other people, and help them respond to you more positively. Optimistic, energetic people are promoted in preference to cynical, inflexible people. So – keep the drive and energy that you have going. If you've lost it – take action to find it again.

Your attitude is the filter through which you see your life. You may not want it rose-coloured, but make it positive! Attitudes change depending on your relationships, the time of year, your time of the month, your level of motivation, the reward in view, or changing events.

What would you say are your basic underlying attitudes?

Head tapes

One way to pin this down further is to be aware of messages you send yourself. These messages are like tapes playing in the back of your mind. They may not originally have been your messages. They may have come from elsewhere: parents, the media, friends, school. In which case, they are part of your conditioning.

> Elaine:
> I've always had my financial independence by working freelance – right through my marriage. It gives me a great feeling of self esteem and comes from my mother drumming into me 'always stand on your own feet!'

> Carla:
> I always approach my work as a Transport Co-ordinator painstakingly and have to do it that bit better than anyone else around me. I think it comes from everyone in my teens telling me that as a black woman I would have to be 10 times as good as anyone else to get anywhere at all.

Here are some head tapes about:

- appearance — 'make sure you always look smart'
- older people — 'your elders are your betters'
- men — 'they enjoy the thrill of the chase'
- other women — 'why don't you behave like Sangeeta?'
- things you do — 'as long as you come out on top'
- things that go wrong — 'that's the day ruined'
- things that go well — 'it was only luck'
- eating — 'finish it up – think of the starving millions'
- attitude — 'you should be content with what you've got'

WHAT ARE YOUR HEAD TAPES?

Write down at least six of your head tapes, and the effect they have had on your life so far:

MEDITATION

Close your eyes. Breathe slowly and easily and let go of any tension that you notice in your body. Let your mind focus on the words 'I am'. Hear them or see them written.

Stay with the words and allow yourself a few minutes of quiet. Let go of any judgement of yourself and aim not to add any further words to make the sentence more complete.

When you start working with this meditation, it is better to focus for two minutes then stop. Then when you are able to stay focussed extend the time deliberately by a few more minutes. Stop by making a clear and deliberate return to the present and then open your eyes.

Summary and action

In this chapter you have done a lot of work on yourself. This provides you with a launch pad for the more outgoing, practical skills chapters later in the workbook. Know yourself and value yourself so that you can become more fully yourself.

Further optional reading

Susan Jeffers – *Feel the Fear and Do It Anyway* – published by Arrow Books
Jenny Morris – *Pride against Prejudice – Transforming attitudes to disability* – published by Women's Press
Angela Mason and Anya Palmer – *Queer Bashing* – published by Stonewall
Hyrum W Smith – *What Matters Most* – published by Simon & Schuster

Action

What are you going to do now to build on the advantages of being you?
What are you going to do to turn the disadvantages into advantages?

Here are some suggestions:

- do something you've never done before
- place yourself in stretching situations
- build your positive attitudes
- consciously stay alert and open to a person different from you
- at the end of every day, identify something new that you've learnt
- take one small step towards meeting one of your values
- associate with people who help you to feel positive

Write yours here:

Specific Action   **By When?**

Profile *Gaye Mallows*

Job Title: Detective Sergeant
Organisation: Cambridgeshire Constabulary

I first decided I wanted to be a police officer at eight years old when the Police visited my primary school. I joined the police at 19 and met my first husband whilst at training school. I got engaged after 10 weeks' training against the advice of family (I was too young) and we married in 1984 after completion of probation. I had to ask my line manager for permission to marry and you weren't allowed a mortgage until you had completed your probation and the house was inspected by the line manager as being suitable for a police officer!

I spent my first year as a uniform patrol officer before joining the shoplifting squad and then support group which was plain clothes duties and dealt with offences such as drugs, prostitution and importuning. I spent a lot of time hanging around male toilets!

Eventually I was asked to move to CID (Criminal Investigation Department) because a female DC (Detective Constable) was on long term sick leave and there was only one other female in the department at that time. I spent a year in the department and was asked to apply for a board to become a DC myself. I duly went along to Force Headquarters for my interview which consisted of three male Detective senior officers. I had prepared well with plenty of examples to give of work I had been involved in only to be asked lots of inappropriate questions such as 'what does your husband think of you going away on a ten week CID course?' and 'how would you cope with over-amorous detectives?'! Needless to say the male candidates weren't asked similar questions and I didn't pass the board.

I continued working in the CID though and stayed there until I became pregnant with my first child when I had to come off reactive duties and work in the staff office. I then became the divisional administrative officer responsible for all petty cash and balancing the books with no prior experience or training.

Eventually I left the force in January 1987 after having to resign as there was no such thing as flexible working or a career break. Three months after the birth of my third child I discovered my husband was having an affair and he decided he 'needed space'. We duly separated and I discovered we were six months in arrears with the mortgage when the Bailiffs turned up at my door. I was left £22,000 in debt, with three children under five and didn't have a job. I decided to do something about it and returned to work as a police officer as I felt that was all I was qualified to do.

I returned to the force in 1993 and had to go back to training school for 15 weeks. With no family living close by and being a single mum I had no choice but to try and employ a live-in nanny. Attempts to find reliable childcare were fraught with difficulties and I had a succession of au pairs – some good, some dreadful. I completed my one year's probationary period in uniform working shifts and then gained a place in the Child Protection Unit. I stayed there for six years during which time I remarried and became pregnant with my fourth child. My husband was also in the force but was signed off on long term sick leave with clinical depression about a month after I found out I was pregnant. Six months later he was out of the job and unemployed.

That time of my life was particularly stressful as I was working full time whilst heavily pregnant and looking after my other children plus my husband who can't actually remember much about that time. After the birth of my little girl I took the statutory 13 weeks maternity leave only and returned to work albeit I had reduced my hours to three days a week.

In August 2000 I started a new job in the training department and stayed there until August 2002 when I was appointed Family Liaison Officer to one of the families involved in the Soham child murders. I stayed on the enquiry until the trial and I can honestly say it was one of the most draining but rewarding enquiries I have ever worked on. Following the Soham enquiry my husband was diagnosed with cancer – the day before my sergeant's exams. I went ahead anyway and am glad to say I passed. My husband had an operation to remove the tumour and then started an intense course of chemotherapy. He didn't find this at all easy which caused problems between him and my eldest son causing me a lot of heartache.

In November 2005 shortly after completing my Springboard course my husband and I separated – it was a difficult decision but one I felt was the right thing to do. We hadn't really communicated for some time and despite me trying to talk about what was going wrong with our relationship he wasn't ready to listen.

We were apart for 11 months and in that time I was promoted to Detective Sergeant and my son came back home to live. I did embark on a new relationship which foundered and caused me to go off work with stress. The one person who came to my rescue at this time was my husband! After much heartache and long conversations we decided to get back together but still live apart. In September 2006 we found out that my husband's cancer had returned and just before Christmas 2006 he had another operation to remove a tumour from his lung before starting another course of chemotherapy.

We are back living together, my eldest son has left home, joined the Navy, completed his initial training before quitting and my eldest daughter has announced she is pregnant and has recently moved out to live with her boyfriend. So I'm going to be a grandmother and I'm only 44! As far as life outside work is concerned, I do have membership to the gym and try and go a couple of times a week although I have slipped somewhat.... I enjoy walking, cycling and get away a few times a year with my family up to the Lake District just to enjoy long walks and tackle some harder ones up places like Hellvellyn. I like going to the cinema and going out for a meal and a chat with my girlfriends which we try and do once every couple of months. I also like to shop – what woman doesn't?!

I'm still here and I still enjoy my job. I don't particularly want to go for further promotion right now but hey, who knows? My advice to any woman in a similar position is follow your instincts and if I can pass an exam and get promoted anyone can.

Learnings

- be prepared to work hard and challenge stereotypes – break the mould
- don't take no for an answer
- support comes from the most unexpected of quarters

4

> *People are like stained glass windows. They sparkle and shine when the sun is out, but when the darkness sets in their true beauty is revealed only if there is a light from within.*
>
> Elisabeth Kübler-Ross

What You've Got Going For You

Objective
- to capitalise on everything you've got going for you for your future action

This chapter is important because

- you need to assess where you shine and where you need polish
- knowing where your strength lies helps you take the next step
- valuing yourself gives you the confidence to tackle things

Contents
- your achievements
- positive and negative forces
- qualities and strengths
- your skills audit
- transferable skills
- your qualifications
- your assertiveness audit
- confidence
- summary and action
- profile of Shereen McQuoid

You have so many aspects of yourself that you could use to achieve your goals. Don't underestimate them, put them to work for you.

Your achievements

Wherever you are on life's path, behind you lie all your achievements and your mistakes too. Before you are your unfulfilled dreams and ambitions.

What achievements in your life are you really proud of? Write at least six. Include any areas of your life – family, work, home, social, sports, hobbies, relationships, community activities, old achievements as well as recent ones.

1.

2.

3.

4.

5.

6.

7.

8.

9.

10.

What is there that you haven't achieved that you may still want to try to achieve? Don't worry at this point about whether they seem achievable or not.

1.

2.

3.

4.

5.

6.

7.

8.

9.

10.

We'll come back to these later.

Positive and negative forces

If you imagine your life as a journey, then what are the forces that are helping you move forward, making it worthwhile and preventing you from being stuck?

Susan: (Positive forces)

My divorce has gone through and I'm in control of my own life again. I need a challenge – I feel under-used. I'm not afraid to try new things, perhaps a change in the type of work I'm doing. I'm keen to make new changes. I've got two very supportive friends. There's got to be more to life than this!

Lai Chan: (Negative forces)

Not being brave enough to climb out of my comfortable rut. Don't want to upset my partner. Afraid of seeming selfish. I hate interviews. Men dominate engineering. Fear of making a fool of myself.

First list all the forces helping you here; everything inside you and outside you. Write down absolutely everything you can think of and ask family, friends or colleagues what they think and add their suggestions even when you don't fully agree with them:

What's holding you back?

Across your path there will be hurdles – they hold you back, deflect you, slow you down, and may even stop you. Getting over them will take some effort on your part.

Lai Chan has mentioned several which were important for her. List all the things that are standing in your way, internal and external, and if you can visualise them, draw pictures of how they appear to you:

Taking control

The exciting and encouraging aspect of this analysis is to realise how much you can influence the hurdles that you've written down. There are very few that are impervious to change. So few that we can identify them here:

- you cannot change your race
- you cannot change your age

But you can change your ATTITUDE to these, and your ways of dealing with the prejudice in others.

You have limited possibilities of transforming:

- society generally
- your company/organisation
- your level of disability
- your gender

But you can change your ATTITUDE to these, by updating your information about them, and being alert to changes. You have the ability to change everything else – if you want to.

Write down things that you want to change about your attitude to yourself:

Qualities and strengths

Knowing your qualities and strengths helps you:

- be confident
- choose appropriate goals
- know when you can achieve goals
- see which situations you will handle well

List your strengths – the things that you feel are your positive qualities – in the top left-hand box. Fill it right up, and be as specific as you can. If your mind has gone a complete blank, talk to your partner, friends, boss and colleagues to get their ideas on what your strengths are.

Now do the same with your weaknesses in the bottom right-hand box. You will be filling in the other two boxes later.

Your strengths	
	Your weaknesses

Strengths and weaknesses are a balancing act

There are no such things as weaknesses, only qualities that are out of balance.

A quality becomes a strength when it is right for you and the situation. A quality becomes a weakness when it is either overdone or underdone for you and the situation.

Look at these examples:

UNDERDONE	QUALITY	OVERDONE
unreliable	reliable	become indispensable
disrespectful	respectful of others	deferential
slow	quick to act	rash
pessimistic	optimistic	impractical/unrealistic
closed mind	open-minded	vague
spineless	determined	ruthless
rigid thinking	being flexible	aimless
indifferent	interested	nosey
unmotivated	ambitious	ruthless
disorganised	organised	obsessive
timid	courageous	foolhardy
timorous	confident	arrogant

Once you have found the potential strength that is being underdone or overdone you will be able to see what kind of action you could take. For example, if you suspect your interest in people overdoes itself to become nosiness, then observe yourself and stop yourself asking those extra questions to satisfy your curiosity.

If you see that your lack of confidence means you appear timorous, find small things with which to push yourself a bit further than you would normally do.

Go back to your chart on page 76 and in the bottom left-hand corner write down the potential strength that you have underlying your out-of-balance 'weaknesses'.

When you've looked at your weaknesses, look back again at your strengths, just to check you are not in danger of overdoing them, and write in the top right-hand corner of the chart on page 76.

Ask someone who knows you well how they see you. Often it is easier for other people to see your strengths than it is for you to see your own, but remember other people's views are just their opinions. They may not have it right – get a second opinion on any doubtful ones. You'll be asking someone else about the skills audit that comes next – you may wish to ask this question at the same time.

MEDITATION

Choose a quality from the last exercise that you know you have or have had in the past. Sit quietly and allow yourself to relax by breathing calmly and rhythmically. Release any tension you feel in your body and then picture in your mind's eye an occasion when you used that quality for positive results.

Think through the scene in as much detail as you can and, if need be, go through the scene two or three times till you have all the detail right, as if you were replaying a video of the scene. Once you have captured all the detail of the positive way in which this quality helped you in the past, imagine that you are able to condense that quality down into a small sphere that you can hold in your hand. Then imagine yourself putting the sphere into a pocket, your purse or handbag; somewhere that you will easily be able to reach it again when you need it.

Now bring yourself back into the room where you are and wriggle your fingers and toes and open your eyes.

Your skills audit

A skill is an ability to do something. You will feel more confident when you are doing things you are already skilled at.

You can assess the level of your ability to do anything and if you have no skill or ability or not enough then you simply have a gap.

Like this:

The next pages have lists of skills for you to rate yourself. Of course, this will be your subjective rating, so before you start, photocopy these pages twice, and ask your manager/work contact and/or a close friend to rate you too. This gives you a comparison and some useful feedback. All of these skills can be related to home life as well as working life.

If you find some skills difficult to rate, try to think of a time in your home or work life when you might have used this skill, or discuss with a friend or colleague what they understand by the skill. The skills listed are general and so you may wish to think of situations where you use or have used them e.g. having ideas in a team meeting even when it's not about your work.

The gaps at the bottom of each category are for you to add any other skills that you want to, such as technical skills specific to your work.

Rate yourself 1 – 5 as follows:

5 – extremely good at this
4 – good at this
3 – OK at this
2 – not too good at this
1 – terrible at this

PLANNING SKILLS

Planning skills are about the future.

Having good planning skills minimises risks and gives a structure to whatever you want to make happen. They enable you to consider possibilities and make decisions. They use your creative and pragmatic qualities. Add your own ideas to the end of the list.

	1 – 5		1 – 5
gathering information	☐	setting objectives	☐
using my imagination	☐	anticipating	☐
visualising what might happen	☐	making decisions	☐
having ideas	☐	exploring and expanding ideas	☐
organising ideas	☐	assessing	☐
diagnosing	☐	interpreting information	☐
categorising	☐		☐
predicting accurately	☐		☐
estimating	☐		☐
budgeting	☐		

DOING SKILLS

Doing skills are about the present. Having made the plan, they get you started and enable you to carry it out. They fall into three categories – in relation to yourself, other people, and things.

1 – 5

using physical strength ☐
using dexterity ☐
computer literate ☐
using co-ordination ☐
motivating others ☐
persuading others ☐
initiating ☐
enthusing ☐
reading ☐
writing ☐
speaking ☐
calculating ☐
observing ☐
using visual awareness ☐
operating machinery ☐
decision making ☐
changing plans ☐
taking risks ☐

1 – 5

understanding instructions ☐
giving instructions ☐
following instructions ☐
attending to detail ☐
prioritising ☐
using time ☐
negotiating ☐
expressing feelings ☐
pacing ☐
seeing steps to be taken ☐
organising resources ☐
add relevant technical
skills here:

☐
☐
☐
☐
☐

KEEPING-GOING SKILLS

Keeping-going skills enable you to sustain action, and also enable you to enjoy things.

	1 – 5		1 – 5
knowing when to stop	☐	having fun	☐
knowing when to keep going	☐	speeding up	☐
encouraging yourself	☐	slowing down	☐
encouraging others	☐	changing plans	☐
laughing	☐	finishing things	☐
creating – words, music, etc.	☐	attending to detail	☐
listening	☐	dealing with conflict	☐
counselling	☐		☐
coaching	☐		☐
helping	☐		☐
using your intuition	☐		☐

EVALUATING SKILLS

Evaluating skills are about getting the best from the past. They enable you to learn, make decisions and make better plans next time.

	1 – 5		1 – 5
assessing objectively	☐	reviewing	☐
measuring results	☐	adapting	☐
comparing results	☐	decision making	☐
observing objectively	☐		☐
letting go	☐		☐
seeing the bigger picture	☐		☐
drawing conclusions	☐		☐

✳

What does it mean?

Got more going for you than you thought? Got less going for you than you thought?

Check that your modesty isn't preventing you boasting a bit or that the perfectionist in you isn't stopping you being satisfied with something that is less than perfect.

How does your own rating compare with that of your manager and/or friend? Do they see you differently?

Use their rating to challenge your own as they may see you more clearly than you see yourself. Who's got it right?

Use this space for your notes of things you've learnt from this exercise:

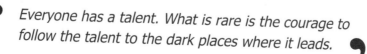

Everyone has a talent. What is rare is the courage to follow the talent to the dark places where it leads.

Erica Jong

Transferable skills

The use of skills is severely limited by putting technical or professional labels on them which lock them into a particular profession. Assessing them under broader headings gives you more flexibility to transfer them to another form of work.

A good secretary can be described as 'just a secretary' or as being very skilled at:

understanding instructions	getting on with people
making decisions	interpreting information
using dexterity	persuading others
using co-ordination	pacing
using visual awareness	breaking things down
using time	organising resources
attention to detail	organising people
working to deadlines	assessing
negotiating	encouraging yourself
computer literacy	encouraging others

Transferring your skills

Women, particularly those who've had a career break or who are unemployed, tend to underrate their skills or not recognise how transferable they are. Make sure you don't do this too.

- skills practised by a call centre worker will transfer into any job dealing with people
- planning and buying for a family can be translated into skills needed by a Store Buyer or Project Manager

> Diane:
> As an unemployed mother of three young children wanting to get back to work, I took a Saturday job at a small supermarket. The manager spotted my potential and asked me to do the stock buying. So I thought about what I bought each week for my family and multiplied it to see what stock I should buy.

Transferring skills for Diane meant that her planning and buying skills needed for a family were translated into skills needed by a store buyer. Equally, the managing skills used by a mother to organise a football party for her nine year old transfer into project management.

Write down one aspect of what you do now in your work or current role. Then write alongside the transferable skills it gives you.

Log your transferable skills on page 273.

 Look at your skills in a transferable way – don't limit yourself.

Your qualifications

Qualifications are rather like theatre or cinema tickets. You have to have them to get you through the door, but once through the door everyone else has a similar ticket. They can also be a double-edged sword, with people regarding you as over-qualified, so either way, qualifications are a powerful message.

Qualifications

- can open doors
- can make it difficult to open doors
- give you credibility

- come in all shapes and sizes
- tell people what you have learnt
- tell people what you can do
- tell people what sort of person you are
- can be an asset or a hindrance
- may be helpful or unhelpful
- educational qualifications diminish in value as you get older
- professional qualifications are often highly valued
- people have got to the top without qualifications

 *If you have qualifications – be proud of your achievements.*

Turn to page 270-271 and log your qualifications under the headings.

If you're thinking you haven't got much written down, don't give up but think about what you may need. Some women have got to the top without formal qualifications, but employers are increasingly looking for qualifications.

The qualifications you had when you left school may have opened some doors. By the time you get to your mid-20s, school-leaving qualifications are no longer relevant: people are looking for more. Similarly, a degree may not mean so much in your 30s as it did in your 20s. You may need to gain more qualifications to suit what you now want to do.

Ways of gaining qualifications

Think about the many ways you can gain qualifications before making future decisions. Award-giving bodies are constantly increasing their flexibility. There are:

- full-time, flexi-time, part-time, block release and short courses
- distance learning, e-learning and Open University-style courses needing little or no time away from home
- evening, day and weekend courses

- fixed schedules and 'take as long as you like' programmes
- National Vocational Qualifications
- internet courses with forums
- computer-based learning packages

Which qualifications?

You don't need any formal qualifications at all to start an Open University degree course. If, on the other hand, you have a PhD, you may still need a vocational qualification to achieve your next goal. Think about the wide range of qualifications before deciding which one to investigate further:

Vocational qualifications e.g.

- Heavy Goods Vehicle Licence
- Public Service Vehicle Licence
- City and Guilds Trade and Supervisory Qualifications
- Certificates in Management
- National Vocational Qualifications
- Police Sergeant's or Inspector's examinations

Academic qualifications e.g.

- GCSEs, GCE, A, AS and A2 levels
- BTEC Certificates and Diplomas for technician and business qualifications
- Degrees: –   Bachelors: BA, BSc
            –   Masters: MBA, MA, MSc, MPhil, LLM, Med
            –   Doctorate: PhD, DPhil

Post graduate and professional qualifications e.g.

- State Registered Nurse
- Membership of Institute of Mechanical Engineers
- Membership of Chartered Institute of Marketing
- Membership of the Chartered Institute of Bankers

There are hundreds of other qualifications to choose from. Take a look at the official government website for the up-to-date information: **www.direct.gov.uk/en/EducationAndLearning/QualificationsExplained**

What qualifications do you want or need to get for your work?

What qualifications do you want to get for your own fun or satisfaction?

Will anyone give you any form of help in getting these qualifications? Your organisation may have a policy to support the gaining of qualifications that are directly related to your work – or unconnected with your work.

Find out if you qualify for support. If you don't know, ask your HR Manager or the person who deals with this in your organisation. If you are not working, or there is no support from your organisation, check other available sources of sponsorship from charitable trusts or even charitable friends. Government initiatives sometimes provide a source of funding. The website above also gives details of possible funding and offers a free call back from a learning advisor.

Your assertiveness audit

Assertiveness is such an important interpersonal skill that we have devoted two chapters of this workbook to it, so you'll be getting a good dose of it later on. Meanwhile, fill in this questionnaire to assess your current level of assertiveness that you have got going for you.

Circle the a, b, c *or* d *response to identify how you tend to behave in these situations. Complete the questionnaire quickly. Your first answers are usually the best and most accurate.*

1. *You would prefer to have Christmas or a similar festival on your own with your partner/friend; your partner wants to go to his/her family. Do you:*

    a. imply that it's unfair and hope things will change?
    b. go to the family – anything for peace?
    c. say how you feel and what you would like?
    d. flatly refuse to go?

2. *You have just started to eat your main course in a restaurant. It should be hot but it's cold. Do you:*

    a. tell the waiter this isn't the item you ordered and order another dish?
    b. carry on and eat it?
    c. tell the waiter it's cold and ask for a fresh hot portion?
    d. point out that this isn't good enough and demand better?

3. *A friend or colleague circulates unwanted emails to you too often. Do you:*

    a. drop hints in polite replies?
    b. delete them and say nothing?
    c. explain the effect on you and ask for them to stop?
    d. fire off an angry email back?

4. *An interview panel member asks a question that seems sexist to you. Do you:*

    a.   quip back a quick retort?
    b.   answer as best you can?
    c.   express some concern about the question only if you feel OK about it?
    d.   point out how wrong it is to ask such questions and refuse to answer?

5. *When you are entering the car park and are about to reverse into a parking space another driver nips in and pinches the space. Do you:*

    a.   block the other car in?
    b.   ignore it and find another space?
    c.   tell the other driver how annoyed you are and ask him/her to move?
    d.   give the other driver a piece of your mind for his/her rudeness?

6. *Someone criticises your appearance. Do you:*

    a.   say something like 'Well it's my most expensive outfit'?
    b.   blush and say nothing?
    c.   check what is specifically being said and judge for yourself?
    d.   tell him/her it's none of his/her business?

7. *You are asked to work late for the third time this week. You already have another appointment. Do you:*

    a.   give what you think is a cast-iron reason for not staying?
    b.   try saying 'no' and end up staying?
    c.   say 'no' firmly and say when you have to leave for your other appointment?
    d.   complain that it's the third time this week and say a definite 'no'?

8. Your family don't seem to be listening when you try telling them about your plans for Saturday. Do you:

a. say something like 'Well if anyone's interested I'm...'?
b. keep quiet?
c. say how you feel and that it's important to you to tell them about your plans?
d. talk more loudly?

9. When you keep quiet in a situation, is it because:

a. you know the silence will have an effect?
b. you are too upset or frightened to speak?
c. you have nothing to say?
d. you're sulking?

10. You feel angry or upset. Do you:

a. let people know in a roundabout way?
b. keep quiet?
c. try to say how you feel and be specific?
d. explode?

Count up how many a's, b's, c's and d's you've scored:

a ☐   b ☐   c ☐   d ☐

Mostly b's

Your behaviour tends to be passive.

Mostly c's

This shows that you tend to be assertive, but check that you actually do the things you say you do. Sometimes it is easy to see what the best solution is on paper but a more passive or more aggressive response may slip out in the heat of the moment.

Mostly a's and d's

Your behaviour tends to be aggressive. The d's are directly aggressive, whilst the a's are indirectly aggressive and manipulative. Most people confuse assertive behaviour with aggressive behaviour, so it's not unusual to have a high score here.

What do you want to change about this pattern?

Confidence

The final part of this chapter is about confidence.

You may have discovered that, while you've got some things going for you, you lack the self-confidence to stick your neck out and get on with it. Or you may feel you haven't the qualities and qualifications, and need the confidence to do something about it.

You may feel confident in work situations and lack confidence in social situations, or the other way round. Everyone's different.

Confidence means

- being able to start things feeling that you will do reasonably well
- you get on with what you want to do
- you feel that whatever happens, you will be OK inside
- being able to have a go even if you're not sure of the outcome

Lack of confidence means

- you feel you can't do things
- you put off doing things till you feel more confident
- you have difficulty doing things
- you feel powerless or uncomfortable, or both
- you feel that whatever you do it won't be good enough
- even when you're doing things well, you feel like a bit of an imposter
- you don't even try

Over-confidence means

- you don't know your own limitations
- you undertake to do things you can't necessarily fulfil
- you are unrealistic

It may be that your reason for working through this book is to help build up your self-confidence. Knowing the situations and people who undermine your self-confidence may give you a clue to the goals you want to set yourself later on in this workbook.

If you are easily intimidated by more senior people you may want to learn assertiveness skills. If you lack confidence in situations when you're asked to speak in public, consider getting on a course about public speaking, or volunteer to do a very short bit of speaking such as making an announcement at a meeting or giving a vote of thanks to a speaker.

CONFIDENCE PEAKS AND TROUGHS

Identify yours here:

I am most confident when:	I am least confident when:
People who help me feel confident are:	People who contribute to my lack of confidence are:
How I can use the confidence I have:	What I can do to build my confidence is:

Use the situations and people who help your confidence as the foundation stones on which to build further confidence. When your confidence takes a knock, remember these situations and use your supporters.

Summary and action

In this chapter, you've looked at many of the things that you've got going for you. Look at all the audits positively and enthusiastically and celebrate all the good things you've got to help you reach your goals. In areas where you are disappointed or deflated, decide firstly whether it matters or not – nobody has everything – and if it does matter, decide what first step you're going to take to do something about it.

Further optional reading

Susan Jeffers – *End the Struggle and Dance with Life* – published by Hodder and Stoughton
Louise Hay – *The Power is Within You* – published by Eden Grove
Petruska Clarkson – *The Achilles Syndrome* – published by Element

Action

What action are you now going to take to develop your skills, strengths, qualifications, and confidence? Here are some suggestions:

- find out about courses
- polish up my listening skills
- ask my boss to explain his/her ratings of my skills
- volunteer to help out and learn about another department/organisation
- get my Workplace Health and Safety Officer's Certificate

Write yours here:

Specific Action   **By When?**

Profile *Shereen McQuoid*

Job Title: Decorator
Organisation: Self Employed

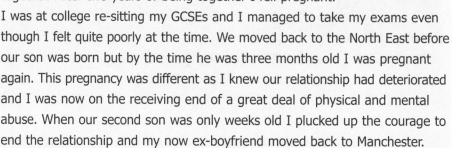

I left school in 1991 without any A-C grade GCSEs.
A few weeks after leaving I met a boy from
Manchester and within six months we were living
together. After two years of being together I fell pregnant.
I was at college re-sitting my GCSEs and I managed to take my exams even
though I felt quite poorly at the time. We moved back to the North East before
our son was born but by the time he was three months old I was pregnant
again. This pregnancy was different as I knew our relationship had deteriorated
and I was now on the receiving end of a great deal of physical and mental
abuse. When our second son was only weeks old I plucked up the courage to
end the relationship and my now ex-boyfriend moved back to Manchester.

This abusive relationship had left me with low self esteem and no confidence.
As a consequence of this I developed an eating disorder which left me pitifully
thin and very weak. A good friend discovered this, helped me to realise what
I was doing to myself and encouraged me to seek help. With help from my
GP and a psychiatrist I was eating better and putting on weight in no time. It
wasn't easy and I just had to take one day at a time.

By the time I was 20 I was a single mother with two kids and I felt like my
life was going nowhere. I really wanted to do something so I enrolled on a
few courses at a local college. The following year, with encouragement from
tutors, I completed an access course. I then applied to a local university and
began a HND in Business and IT. Whilst there I struck up a relationship with a
fellow student and completed the course in 2000. We both decided to carry
on and complete a full degree but in my final year I became pregnant again
and was so ill that I had to leave. My boyfriend carried on with his degree
and our son was born a few weeks before he graduated.

When our son was about six weeks old we attended a jobs fair so my newly
graduated boyfriend could look for a job. He left with no job leads – but I'd

enrolled on a teacher training course which was one night a week at a local college. I was given a teacher placement and was offered a part-time job within a few weeks. For three and a half years I worked for a community team travelling all over the East Durham area. My hours reduced and I decided I'd rather spend some time at home with our youngest son before he reached school age.

One day I spoke to a friend who mentioned she was setting up her own business and asked if I was interested in doing the same. As my youngest son was now at nursery, I gave it some thought and decided to set up a decorating business – I'd decorated for my dad whilst at university. I was offered help from various agencies and successfully completed a three-month course for new business start ups. A grant was given to help with business start up costs and I began trading in April 2005.

My business has now been running for a year and a half and is doing very well. As well as decorating interiors and exteriors I also give advice and guidance on materials, colours and soft furnishings. I also tile, fit basic kitchens and lay flooring. I mainly work alone but when needed my brother and dad help out. I work within a half hour driving radius from my home and I do both domestic and commercial work. I seem to be popular with women, especially the elderly, as they feel more comfortable with a woman in their home than a man. I have recently become qualified in painting and decorating to a NVQ Level 2.

Many people find it unusual that I enjoy and carry out this type of work. The business fits in with my family life and I have all of the school holidays off with the children. It's a big change from my teaching career but very enjoyable. However, I have started teaching again for a few hours a week as I did miss my students.

I look back at how my life was 10 years ago and it seems unrecognisable – I was a single mother with two kids and no prospects. I'm now happily married to my boyfriend from university with three sons and a good life ahead of me. I've come so far and this is down to my determination to make something of my life along with the help and support I have received from my friends and family. My mum, in particular, has provided me with childcare over the past 10 years and I really appreciate and value this.

Learnings

- the support of friends and family is hugely important
- take a lead from those who encourage you
- be alert to new opportunities
- personal skills can become professional skills

> ‘ *Too many people let others stand in their way and don't go back for one more try.* ’

Rosbeth Moss Kanter

Who Have You Got Going For You?

Objectives
- to identify how other people may help or hinder you
- to maximise support from your relationships

This chapter is important because

- only a very few of us make it on our own
- you can encourage other people to support you

Contents
- how people influence you
- the roles people play
- networking and building your contacts
- summary and action
- profile of Lullyn Tavares

Making relationships that support you

None of us lives in a vacuum. You may be all too well aware of the influence other people have had on you, or you may feel that you've done it all on your own. Being aware of the effect of other people on you can help you find support.

How people influence you

The influence that other people have can vary enormously:

- directly or indirectly
- negatively or positively
- consciously or unconsciously

Influences that appeared negative at the time, in retrospect, can prove positive:

'Being determined to make a success of my career was the only way I knew of delaying the marriage I knew my parents wanted for me.'

'Going back to work because of a divorce, and re-discovering a career that I really love.'

Active Goodwill

If you could think of everyone you are acquainted with (and research shows that we all can know about 500 people) they are likely to fall broadly into three categories along a scale of 'helpfulness'.

- 10% are people who will actively help you – no matter what
- 80% are people who aren't particularly interested in you, but would help, if you took the initiative
- 10% are people who don't like you, or what you stand for, and will actively hold you back or try to stop you

The 10% who are for you already – they like you and will actively support you, give you ideas and contacts, and encourage you. Keep them in the picture about your plans. You text, e-mail and ring each other quite often and meet up and you feel good about your relationship with them.

The 10% who are against – you won't win everyone over, so it may be a waste of time and energy trying to turn these people round.

The huge majority of people you know will be in the 80% in the middle. These people can be described as having 'latent goodwill' towards you. They do not lie awake at night worrying about you, but equally are not going to slip banana skins under your feet. They probably don't think about you at all! These people are important to you – it is your job to turn their latent goodwill into active goodwill. You'll have to take the initiative here.

Marjorie:
An old school friend used to work in a bank before she took a career break. I'm thinking of setting up my own business and therefore I would need a small loan. So I decided to pick her brains about how to go about it. She was very helpful, gave me lots of tips on preparing my case and helped me to realise that an overdraft facility might be appropriate. I feel when I go to see the bank manager I'll be better able to talk 'bank language'.

 It's up to you to take the first step, to know which battles to fight, and which to leave alone.

The roles people play

A useful way of looking at people is in terms of the role they play in our lives, while remembering that one person may play several roles – often all at once!

The next exercise is to help you identify the ways in which people influence or help you at present, and to identify any gaps. If you already have ideas for your future think also about how they could help you take the next steps.

Write the names of people you know under each category and make a few notes about why they are there:

1 ENERGY GIVERS – PEOPLE WHO MAKE YOU FEEL GOOD

We all need these people – they give you the warmth and reassurance to keep going when life gets tough, and give comfort when you fail. Their warmth restores you. They are easy to be with. They boost your confidence because you know they are on your side.

2 ENERGY DRAINERS – PEOPLE WHO DRAIN YOUR ENERGY

These people don't realise the effect they have on you, but being with them either makes you feel ineffective and frustrated, or exhausted and apathetic. They may be very nice, well-meaning people, but they take away your energy to achieve your goals. They may be bright and chatty or dull and gloomy. They take up too much of your time and sap your confidence.

3 ROLE MODELS – PEOPLE WHO HAVE SET THE PRECEDENT

These are the people who have done what you are thinking of doing and against whom you may be compared. They can be a positive influence, such as opening up new areas for women in the world of work, or negative, such as setting standards of behaviour which you won't follow.

4 HEROES AND HEROINES – PEOPLE WHO INSPIRE YOU

These may be people you know personally and could also be people who you don't know – alive or dead, real or fictitious. They contribute to your sense of purpose and your determination, and help you see where your goals for the future lie or inspire ideas of who you may become.

5 GATEKEEPERS – PEOPLE WHO CONTROL YOUR ACCESS TO OPPORTUNITIES

These people control your access to training, information, resources, people, support, and ideas, and they mostly like to have recognition for doing this. It may be their job to do so – Line Managers and HR Managers may fall into this category. Family and friends open and shut doors too. Gatekeepers can be helpful or unhelpful and can be more senior or more junior than you.

6 Neutral People – Those who will help if you ask them

These are the people who aren't particularly interested in you, but will help if you take the initiative. You will have to ask for their advice, ideas and information, but they will be quite happy to give it. This is likely to be a large category and may overlap with many of the others. They are not telepathic so you will need to tell them what you want.

7 Enemies – People who actively oppose your progress

These people don't like you, or what you stand for, may resent your success or feel threatened by or jealous of what you're trying to do. You may not have anyone opposing you quite as strongly as this but you may know of people on the edge of this role. Enemies put you down, undermine the support you get from others and the confidence you build up.

8 Gardener Bosses, coaches or mentors – People who grow you

These are the bosses who have a reputation for giving people opportunities and for stretching them. After that it's up to you. Grab the opportunities they offer to speed up your development! Gardener bosses enjoy helping others to develop and grow – get all the support you can from them when you have one – and look for one if you haven't got one. Think also about others who coach or mentor you whether formally or informally.

9 APPRENTICES – PEOPLE YOU ARE HELPING AND ENCOURAGING

Who are you opening doors for or helping up behind you? Who looks to you for encouragement and may regard you as a mentor or coach? Your relationship with them helps you to develop. Both in and outside of work, developing your successors may free you up to do new things.

> ❝ *Always remember that you are not the only one who has ever felt rejected, unloved and lonely at some time. Reach out and help someone else in trouble, and you could be amazed at the changes in yourself – and your life!* ❞
>
> Anon.

HOW DOES THIS HELP?

Are you getting enough objective advice and feedback? Are you being challenged enough? Are you getting enough support? Do you need a mentor or coach? Is your access to information and ideas wide enough, or are all your ideas coming from one area?

To get the best out of the previous exercise, think about these questions:

Which, if any, categories predominate?

How do you feel about this?

Which, if any, categories are totally missing?

What do you want to do about this?

Where is your main help and support coming from?

Who is giving you constructive feedback?

How will you deal with those who are hindering you?

❝ *A brain to pick, a shoulder to cry on, and a kick in the pants.* ❞

Natasha Josefowitz – *Paths to Power*

MEDITATION

Relax and release any tension in your body. Allow your breathing to settle and take you to a deeper state of relaxation. Breathe evenly and deeply.

Think about the qualities of a person who is really supportive. You may use a real person who has already supported you, a famous person, someone from films or fiction or a mixture of several people who, if rolled into one, would be the most supportive person that you can imagine.

Take your time building the picture and thinking about the person. Now imagine yourself having a brief conversation with that person to ask her or him for support for the changes that you are going to make in your life.

Imagine that she or he replies very positively but also with an eye to the reality of what you may embark on next. So she or he will gently challenge you as well as support if it seems as if you need to be challenged.

Close by assuring yourself that if you ever want to get support or advice from this imaginary person all you have to do is to sit or lie quietly and tune in to the image you have now created.

Open your eyes and bring yourself gently back into the present by counting how many different colours there are around you. (This is simply to make sure that you are back in reality after being in your imagination.)

FURTHER OPTIONAL WORK

To take this further, you can look at this exercise in reverse and explore the roles that you play in other people's lives. Are you being cast in the same role too often? Do you want to change the balance of the roles you're in?

Networking and building your contacts

Here we are using 'networking' to mean a positive process of mutual support. Extending your contacts to give you greater access to ideas, people, support and opportunities is extremely positive and influential.

Your own network is simply everyone you know. If you extend that to everyone they know, your network multiplies many times again.

Sometimes we know people because we like them just for their own sake and sometimes because of an existing connection or a mutual interest e.g. family, neighbours, fellow professionals, members of internet networks/ chat rooms, people with the same sports, hobbies or interests.

The more people you know, the greater your flexibility to achieve your goals. You do not have to become friends with everyone, indeed you may not even like them. Knowing people is rather like travel – it broadens the mind!

Formal networks

In addition to getting to know people informally, there are hundreds of more formal networks, ranging from Parent Teacher Associations, through to professional institutes and women's groups. See Chapter 14 for details of some of these networks. This is just the tip of the iceberg, so do some detective work and you will find many more. If there isn't a branch of what you need in your area, start one! Most of these groups started with one or two women getting together casually, and building it up from there.

HOW WELL ARE YOUR CONTACTS WORKING?

Use this grid to form your action points from this chapter:

	What is working well	What action to improve?	By when?
Generally			
Up-to-date contacts			
Out-of-date contacts			
Meeting people very different to you			
Meeting people who know things that are helpful for your future			
At work			
Your email contacts			
Your text/phone contacts			
Your face-to-face contacts			
Contacts in other departments			

	What is working well	What action to improve?	By when?
Outside of work Your email contacts			
Your text/phone contacts			
Your face-to-face contacts			
Who you send cards to at birthdays and festivals – Christmas, Divali, Eid, New Year etc.			
Formal networks/ organisations List the ones you belong to and then assess them			

Don't underestimate people – they mostly want to help.

Further optional reading

Lily Segerman-Peck – *Networking and Mentoring* – published by Piatkus

Summary and action

In this chapter, you've taken a brief look at the role and influence of other people in your life, and how you can build on that positively. You have already been networking but you may want to do this more consciously in the future.

Action

What other action will you take now to help people to help you?
For example:

- search the internet for local women's networks
- ask someone I admire about their career path
- contact an old friend
- ask my boss for straight feedback
- talk to someone in a different department about what they do there
- let go of a redundant relationship

If anything is not included in the table above, add it here:

Profile *Lullyn Tavares*

Job Title: Administration and Projects Officer
Organisation: Age Concern, England

I was born in Grenada, spice island of the Caribbean, invaded by the United States in 1983 and more recently caught up in the eye of the storm (Hurricane Ivan The Terrible) in September 1994, swiftly followed by Hurricane Emily. When my brothers and I were little, my mother had always stubbornly remained in her own house – then a wooden house – whenever there was a 'hurricane alert' rather than seek shelter in the nearest school or brick building. So I wasn't surprised to hear that as Ivan huffed and puffed towards this small volcanic island, she didn't stir, but watched the whole thing on TV before communication was lost. My father prayed. The roof caved in and missed them both by inches – my sons tell me that I'm just like Grandma!

I was 11 years old when my mother and I joined my father who was already in England. Caribbean people were actively enticed to migrate to the UK at this time and lots of my friends and family were emigrating, so it wasn't such a wrench to leave as we met up again at social functions. I enjoyed attending school with pupils from different parts of the world, but I was worried then (still do) about the low level of education and expectations in some of our schools.

I did various secretarial jobs after leaving school, and then whilst working at a solicitor's firm decided to do a BA degree with the Open University, with ideas of becoming a teacher or doing some sort of counselling work with children. A much admired Scottish teacher had tried his best to persuade me and a couple of my friends to become teachers. 'There will be a great need for good black teachers' he advised even then.

A very clever and ambitious chemistry student came into my life and we enjoyed a carefree period. After his PhD he gained a year's sabbatical at the University of Bordeaux with a small apartment nearby. By then I had finished my degree and I joined him until returning to England for the birth of our first son. When my husband returned to England, we started a Research and

Development business, which was very hard work for over eight years but scientifically ground-breaking and rewarding. During that time we also had another two sons.

Despite some scientific breakthrough, it was difficult to raise the funds we needed, so we mortgaged the house as collateral for the business. High interest rates and other problems set in. The bank wanted closure, pressured us into selling up and we became homeless. This period was difficult. Finding a reasonable place to live at affordable prices wasn't (and still isn't) easy. Yoga and pottery classes, good friends and family kept me focused. Our first priority was stability and education of our children which meant remaining close to their school, friends, Boys Brigade, grandparents and family.

By then I had acquired a diploma in management (also with the Open University). I updated my administration and secretarial skills, found work and negotiated the pay and hours to suit our circumstances. My husband and I have always shared looking after the children and the housework and I'd always found time to do other things. Voluntary work, being a school governor, playgroup and nursery school leader all provided opportunities for learning and improving my skills, which boosted my CV considerably.

I have been working as an administration and projects officer in the Research and Development Unit at Age Concern England for a number of years now. This is a well-known Charity to promote the wellbeing of all older people and help make later life a fulfilling and enjoyable experience. I've always felt strongly against inequality and discrimination and this is an area of work I find very interesting. I think age discrimination and lack of respect and services for some older people is appalling and it gives me great satisfaction to do my bit to high-light these issues. There is now an increasing older minority ethnic population in the UK which is another interesting dimension to the work that I do.

It's not all paperwork though! I've recently acquired an ITEC diploma in anatomy and physiology at evening classes, and also trained to be an EXTEND teacher. EXTEND is a charity which provides recreational movement to music for the over-60s and less able people of all ages. Whenever possible, I take classes. I like dancing and encourage my class to dance, (even sitting down!) and to have a laugh despite some of their physical difficulties. Movement to music is a healthy and enjoyable activity to do, at whatever age, whenever you want to perk yourself up. I have done some Reiki training and intend to take courses in holistic massage and reflexology, now that my children are away at university, so that I can become a practitioner when I'm no longer working full-time.

Learnings

- be clear about your priorities
- do voluntary work. You will enjoy it, make new friends and gain additional skills
- make sure your work interests you

> *I make my own decisions and couldn't imagine anyone else doing that, because I am in control of my own destiny. And if anything happens, or if a mistake is ever made, it's because it's something I chose to do.*

Janet Jackson

Setting Your Goals

Objectives
- to build on your successes
- to set your goals

This chapter is important because

- goals give you a sense of direction
- goals keep you moving
- goals determine what you do next
- goals channel your energy

Contents
- goals
- think-through questionnaire
- building on your successes
- vision and sense of direction
- the time of your life
- setting your goals
- is it worth it?
- what are you waiting for?
- summary and action
- profile of Sue Matthews

In this chapter you will be setting your goals, drawing on the work you've already done. The goals can be as ambitious or cautious as you wish, as personal or work-related as you wish, as public or private as you wish. People who set and document goals and take action are generally happier and better off than those who don't.

Goals

- help clarify your thoughts
- get you started
- save time
- give you the impetus to make changes
- are not set in concrete and can be changed!

Some people feel uncomfortable about setting goals because:
- it seems like tempting fate
- if they don't reach them, they'll feel a failure
- if they're a success – what next?
- they'd rather just let life happen to them
- they're too busy
- they don't have the confidence

How do you feel about setting your goals?

Think-through questionnaire

Life for many women is rather like doing a circus balancing act while juggling at the same time! For those setting out on adult life there are so many options to think about and choices to make. Older women have to take account of the consequences of many previous decisions. Take as much time as you need to think about the questions that are important to you.

The questions are designed to help you think about the different aspects of your life. Use them to clarify your thoughts and spark off ideas to help you in your goals. Skip the sections that don't apply to you.

Money matters

Money matters a great deal to some and not to others. Consider:

- do you have your own income?
- if so, how well does your income match your outgoings?
- how do you feel about the difference?
- are you the only breadwinner? What does this mean to you?
- do you have, or are you considering having, a mortgage?
- how much more do you want to earn?
- how much less could you manage on if you really needed to or wanted to?
- how much money do you want to earn long-term?
- what about a pension? Do you have one? Is it the best one for you?
- do you have any investments or savings? Do you know what's best for your future investment?
- what if you became ill or couldn't work for a long time?
- do you need help to sort out your debts?

Work circumstances

Are you in paid employment?
Are you looking for paid employment?
How do you feel about working/not working in paid employment?

How do you want to work?

- full-time?
- part-time?
- flexi-time?
- job-sharing?
- self-employment or contract working?
- teleworking from home?

How prepared are you to move for work?

- what daily travelling are you prepared to do?
- how far would you move for the right opportunity?
- how much does your current pension scheme (if you have one) influence your decision to change work?

If you are thinking of starting your own business, or already have one, consider:

- how far down the track are you?
- what is the nature of your product or service?
- what market are you in?
- who specifically are your customers?
- what do they buy now?
- who are your competitors?
- how will market trends affect your business?
- how will you cope if your income is irregular?

Living on your own

- is it out of choice, or through circumstances?
- what do you enjoy most about living on your own?
- what do you like least about living on your own?
- how long do you want to go on living on your own?
- what do your friends/family think about it?
- do they pressurise you to do something different?
- how does it affect you financially?
- what do you like to do for holidays?

Considering a close partnership

If you are considering sharing your life with someone else, do you:

- see it as a partnership for life or short-term?
- want to live with the person?
- know where you will live?
- want to share financial arrangements?
- want to make it a legal arrangement (marriage, civil partnership, trust deed)?

- want to have sex with them?
- feel your freedom being eaten away?
- know what you want out of the relationship?
- know what the other wants?
- know your doubts, fears and hopes?
- share your doubts, fears and hopes with the other?
- love the person? (Or are you in love? Or both?)
- know how compatible or complementary your daily rhythms are?
- know how your work patterns relate to each other's?
- know what effect it will have on your social life?
- know how your track record with relationships is influencing you?

Being in a partnership

- how do you feel about your relationship?
- how much respect does your partner show for you?
- to what extent does your sex life satisfy you?
- to what extent do you tolerate verbal, emotional or physical abuse?
- what financial arrangements do you have – separate or joint bank accounts, credit cards, etc?
- how do you share all the expenses: equally? Proportionate to your income? Pool everything and treat it as if it's one income?

If your partner earns less than you or is not in paid employment, do you:

- treat all income as joint?
- make clear the differences?
- try to compensate by paying for things quietly or secretly?
- never mention it?
- feel OK about it – or not OK?
- know how your partner really feels about it?

If you earn less than your partner or are not in paid employment, also look at the questions above.

If you both work

What comes first?

- your work?
- your partner's work?
- your relationship with each other?

How do you see your own work?

- essential financially?
- unimportant for your fulfilment as a person?
- necessary for your development as a person?
- gets in the way of your relationship?
- enhances your relationship?
- stops you being effective in other roles?
- helps you cope with other roles?

How does your partner see your work?

- essential financially?
- unimportant for your fulfilment as a person?
- necessary for your development as a person?
- gets in the way of your relationship?
- enhances your relationship?
- stops you being effective in other roles?
- helps you cope with other roles?

How mobile/flexible are you and your partner?

- will move for own work?
- will move for your partner's work?
- happy to be away for short / longer spells?
- happy for each other to be away for short / longer spells?
- whose work takes priority?

What about holidays?

- have them together?
- have them separate?
- it varies?

How long do you see your partnership lasting?

- forever?
- for quite some time?
- ending soon?

Considering having children?

- how do you feel about it?
- how does your partner (if you have one) feel?
- what size family do you want?
- how will having children affect your life generally (financially, practically, emotionally)?

What will be the effects on your work of having children?

- types of work?
- mobility?

What arrangements will be needed for times of ill health?

Who will take what amount of time off around the birth?

Will you and/or your partner take a career break?

How might a career break affect:

- your career?
- your life with the child(ren)?
- your partnership?

What arrangements are needed for childcare?

How does being a working mother appeal to you?

What do you enjoy or look forward to about being a working mother?

What if you are unable to have children?

- how might you feel?
- what help will you seek?
- when will you give up trying?
- will you consider adoption?

No children?

- is this a conscious choice?
- how do you feel about it?
- what are the benefits and drawbacks?
- how do other people treat you as a result?
- what might change this situation?

Already have children?

Who supports the child(ren) financially?

If you are a working mother, how is that for you?

How do/would you cope with the child(ren) or your partner in the event of:

- illness in the family?
- short spells away for work?
- longer spells away for work?

Who cares for your child(ren) after school and in the school holidays?

If your child is under school age, how happy are you with your childcare arrangements?

Who arranges childcare?

Who does the 'thinking' about how the child(ren) are looked after?

What do you need to do to improve things?

Does your child have any special needs?

How does this affect your life?

How is your relationship with your child(ren) changing as they grow up?

How do you feel about your child(ren) leaving or having left home?

How does having grown-up child(ren) affect you?

Dependent relative?

What effect does this situation have on your life?

- financially?
- emotionally?
- in terms of time?
- in terms of mobility?

What special needs does your relative have?

How much are you able to meet the needs yourself?

How are the rest of the needs met?

What support services are available to you?

What further support do you still need?

What changes do you foresee in the immediate future?

How could an organisation's career break scheme help?

Philosophy of life

Everybody has one, whether it is a deeply held spiritual or religious belief or a catch phrase you run your life by, such as 'Live and let live', or 'Never do harm to anyone'. It may not be something you think about every day.

- what is your philosophy of life?
- what is your faith, religion or spiritual belief?
- if none, what is your view – agnostic, atheist?
- do you follow any other particular path of development?
- what are you looking for or hoping for?
- what are your views about death?
- have you made a Will? If not, why not?
- how much does all of this influence your daily life?

WHAT DOES ALL THIS MEAN?

You have now reviewed some of the personal circumstances about your life which affect your decisions for the future. Jot down here what has come out of this:

What surprises were there (if any)?

What questions needed the most thought?

What needs more thought before you set your goals?

What do you need to discuss with others before you set your goals?

What do you want to change?

Discuss any issues that have arisen from this think-through questionnaire with the people involved or someone who can help you digest the questions and answers that have been provoked.

Building on your successes

Before you set your goals, one more aspect will influence them – your track record and view of success. Whenever you feel successful, it boosts your confidence and spurs you on.

What does success mean to you?

Jot down ideas of what success is for you – add at least five ideas:

Success is
Success is
Success is
Success is
Success is
Success is
Success is
Success is
Success is
Success is

WHAT DOES IT MEAN?

Each woman has her own personal blend of definitions of success. Check that yours are specific, e.g. to write 'success is being happy' is very general – what do you mean by 'being happy'?

Notice how many of them you are already achieving.

My definition of success for me:

Vision and sense of direction

You may already be very clear about what you want to do (that may be why you're working with this workbook), but if you're not, consider two different approaches – being a person who has a vision, or a person who has a sense of direction.

Vision

Some people are natural visionaries. They often see things in their heads, and can actually describe the picture to others. Others may have a vision of how life could be which drives them on (of a social injustice put right, or a world based on different values). It is this vision which inspires and energises them so they are motivated by achieving, in whatever measure, the vision that they have. Have a go at being a visionary:

YOUR VISION OF THE FUTURE

Let go of any doubts, hurdles, fears or thoughts. In a consciously optimistic frame of mind, build a picture that is as detailed and as positive as you can make it. Let yourself go and let your imagination run riot. Imagine how you would like a day in your life to be in five years' time and use the questions on the following pages to give you some ideas. Deliberately go over the top with your picture.

Jot down notes
or...
Write the story of it, like a magazine article
or...
Tell the story to someone else as if it was what you are going to do tomorrow

or...

Paint the picture – take a large sheet of paper and paint or colour your future day in any way you like.

Think about:

Where are you? Which country, town, village? What sort of place, building, countryside? How is the scene? Well kept, desolate, palatial?

What are you doing?

Who's with you?

What is fulfilling about your life?

What fun are you having?

Why is it fun?

What are you good at?

How do you feel about it?

The answers to any of these questions could become goals.

> " *If you have built castles in the air, your work need not be lost: that is where they should be. Now put foundations under them.* "

Henry David Thoreau

Sense of direction

Other people have no vision, but are equally motivated by a commitment to a WAY of doing things, which gives them a strong sense of direction. They know which way to go and how to make choices day-to-day. They know that if they are prepared they will be ready to take opportunities as they arise.

If you're more a 'direction' type of person, or are still unsure of your overall goals, then consider these questions to sharpen up your direction:

What makes you really angry?

What do you get really excited about?

If you were to die today, what would you regret not having achieved?

What ambitions do you have that remain unfulfilled? Think back to your childhood ambitions – any unfulfilled ambition will give you clues.

What unfulfilled dreams do you have, no matter how crazy or outlandish?

What are your deepest held values? See page 61. Are they being met?

Are you spending the time of your life as you would wish? If not, what do you want to do about it?

The time of your life

If your answer to the last question was 'No' then take another look at how you're spending your time now.

The circle on the next page represents all your time and energy excluding sleeping, and you could include sleep if that is an issue for you. Think about three categories of use for this time and energy. You can subdivide these main categories if you want to; these are just to get you started.

WORK = time spent on your paid or unpaid employment or full-time education

HOME = time spent on maintaining the home and family, i.e. looking after children, duties, chores, visiting relatives

LEISURE = time spent on yourself or doing things you enjoy (this includes your 'me time')

Divide the circle into proportions that show how you'd generally LIKE life to be:

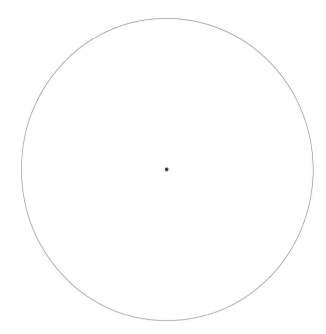

Now repeat the same exercise, dividing up the circle into how it actually is at the moment. Take an overview of how it feels, don't start doing elaborate time logs!

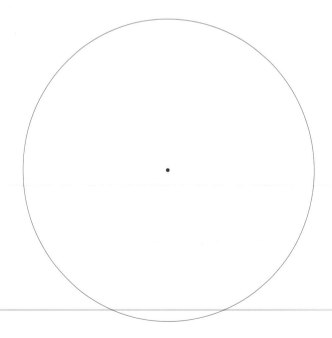

Take a look at what you've drawn – where are the conflicts between the two circles? While it's fresh in your head, jot down the aspects of your use of time that you'd like to change. These may spur you on and become goals.

The dream/reality gap

Between the dreams of the future and the reality of the present there is often a gap. If the gap seems very big or insurmountable then it puts people off trying. When you look at the gap you can:

- find choices where there appears to be no choice
- look for the first simple steps to take you in the right direction
- challenge your assumptions about your constraints

 You have much more freedom than you think.

Setting your goals

 Take your dream seriously. You are here to become the best you can be. You owe it to yourself.

Susan Hayward – *Begin It Now*

Set whatever goals you want to:
- short-term and long-term
- serious and more light hearted
- connected with work and connected with home
- just for you and involving other people
- outrageous and conventional
- upfront and secret
- within your current organisation and outside of it
- within the familiar and going out into the unknown

One good tip is to set a mixture – it will make life more interesting, and when you get stuck with one you can take action on another.

Follow the charts on the next pages. They break into four categories:
- goals at work
- goals in your relationships
- goals just for you
- goals to help the world

*In the **first column** put the overall goal – just a line or two on your overall objective.*

*In the **second column** break the goal down into all the small, individual actions you will have to take to achieve the goal – be as detailed as you can. For example, to achieve this goal:*
- what skills will you need?
- what qualifications will you need?
- how much money will you need?
- what relationships will you need?
- what motivation and determination will you need?
- what will you need to change in yourself?
- what will you have to give up, in order to achieve this?
- what information will you need?

*In the **third column**, consider the possible consequences for you and other people if you choose this goal.*

Have a go – after all you're not carving in granite – it's just a bit of paper and you can always change it!

YOUR GOALS AT WORK

Goal	Action needed – by when	Possible consequences for me and others

YOUR GOALS IN YOUR RELATIONSHIPS

Goal	Action needed – by when	Possible consequences for me and others

YOUR GOALS JUST FOR YOU

Goal	Action needed – by when	Possible consequences for me and others

YOUR GOALS TO HELP THE WORLD

Goal	Action needed – by when	Possible consequences for me and others

MEDITATION – TO ENERGISE YOU

Find a quiet spot and sit down or lie down and begin by breathing out through your nose a little bit extra on the next out breath. Let your breathing settle and see if you can notice the difference in the air as it flows from your nostrils over your upper lip. It may be colder as it goes in and warmer as it comes out.

Now imagine your body being covered by the colours of the rainbow going from your head, where your goals and visions begin, to your feet which take you forward into action:

Start at the top of your head with violet.
Next imagine your brow with indigo or a very deep blue.
Then on to your throat with blue.
Going down further to your heart area with green.
Then place yellow just below your waist in your solar plexus.
Moving to orange in the area below your tummy button.
Finally to red in your genital area and on down your legs to your feet.

To finish, sit or stand up if you are lying down, stand if you are sitting and stamp your feet a few times.

Is it worth it?

Having set your goals, look back at what you've written, think about the consequences of all the hard work you've committed yourself to, and ask yourself the one last question: Is it worth it?

If the answer is 'No' then you have set inappropriate goals, set them too high, or with inappropriate deadlines. Go back and amend your sheets until the answer is 'Yes', because the answer has to be 'Yes' for you to carry on.

Reaching 'YES' means you've reached the point of commitment. It's one thing to write down goals and know what you want to do with them. It's another matter to get started and keep going. That takes commitment.

Commitment:

- turns ideas into action
- changes wishes into intentions
- takes courage and determination
- has to be renewed each day
- means you put your energy into it

This is the point to take the plunge and commit to action or go back and work through earlier parts of the process again.

What are you waiting for?

- the children to leave home/start school?
- the boss to retire?
- to win the Lottery?
- someone to encourage you?
- someone to make it safe for you?
- to lose weight?
- to feel ready?
- someone to die?
- someone to give you permission?
- a kick?
- someone to explain technology to you?
- to get your qualification?
- the perfect job?
- to stop feeling guilty?
- your knight in shining armour?
- to stop feeling frightened?

It's easy to stop yourself setting goals or taking steps to achieve them if you think you have a good reason not to do it now. There may be very valid reasons why you cannot do something now, but just check that it's a real reason and not an excuse.

You may be working through this workbook because you feel you don't have any goals, so if you *still* feel that you don't have a goal, then setting a goal becomes your goal.

One way to help your commitment to your goals is to share them with someone who will support and encourage you. Have a conversation with someone you can trust to strengthen your commitment.

 Don't be afraid to take a big step if one is indicated. You can't cross a chasm in two small jumps.

David Lloyd George

Having done that – stop

You have now achieved what for many people is the most difficult part of personal development – setting goals. Having the imagination and the determination to decide what to do is half the battle.

Now you've decided what you're going to do, the next step is to find how to do it. Make the process enjoyable.

 It is not how things turn out – it's the joy of doing it!

Barbra Streisand

Before you move on, have a celebration – whatever you like. Award yourself a treat – an evening off, a long bubble bath, a walk with a special friend – anything!

It's important that you acknowledge the importance of what you've just done.

A JOURNEY OF 1,000 MILES STARTS WITH A SINGLE STEP

Anon.

Summary and action

In this chapter, you've been asked to consider a great number of issues. You've thought about whether you have vision or direction, and you've set your goals.

Further optional reading

Look for inspiration in the biographies of others.

Action

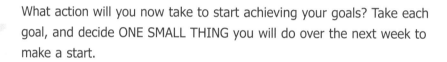

What action will you now take to start achieving your goals? Take each goal, and decide ONE SMALL THING you will do over the next week to make a start.

 Nothing is too small to be a start.

Write yours here:

Specific Action   **By When?**

Profile *Sue Matthews*

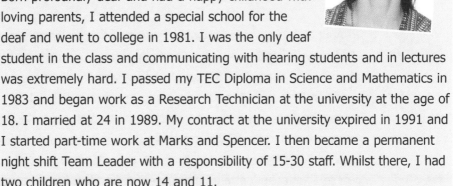

Job Title: Research Technician
Organisation: Leeds University

Born profoundly deaf and had a happy childhood with loving parents, I attended a special school for the deaf and went to college in 1981. I was the only deaf student in the class and communicating with hearing students and in lectures was extremely hard. I passed my TEC Diploma in Science and Mathematics in 1983 and began work as a Research Technician at the university at the age of 18. I married at 24 in 1989. My contract at the university expired in 1991 and I started part-time work at Marks and Spencer. I then became a permanent night shift Team Leader with a responsibility of 15-30 staff. Whilst there, I had two children who are now 14 and 11.

In 1997 I was considered for a Cochlear Implant to enable me to hear but due to lack of support from my now ex-husband I did not have the confidence to have the operation and so I declined the offer.

In 2001 I got myself a part-time job back at the university. However, after the first morning in my new job the next day my husband left me, without any explanation, to cope with two small children aged seven and five, home and a new job. Without any hearing at all – alone in a house where I could not hear if my children called out in the night. A silent world. My mother was left to contact the university to explain my circumstances. I was very fortunate that they were understanding and offered to keep my job open until I was ready to return. I sought the advice of a solicitor with the help of my mum who has supported me through thick and thin. In the end I had to go to court to fight for my financial needs but I got a social worker from the deaf club to help me in communicating with solicitors and courts.

At the lowest point of my life, I had a complete nervous breakdown. My doctor referred me to a psychologist and I had counselling sessions. I also had to have a premature hysterectomy that was brought on by aggravated stress. After only one month, I went back to work meeting new people once again.

Slowly, I began to re-build my life after 11 years of marriage and coping with my daughter having frequent nightmares asking why daddy had left. My divorce came through in 2003 and it was a bitter blow for me. I then had a bad bout of flu which further affected the little hearing I had with hearing aids. I became even more isolated and I reached levels of extreme frustration when trying to communicate with my children and with adults.

In April 2005 I attended a women's development programme run at the University under licence from The Springboard Consultancy. I knew I should attend and arranged for signers to be present for the duration of the sessions. Throughout the programme, I started to rebuild my confidence, self-esteem and assertiveness. During the first session I gave a short presentation to other delegates – it was not easy with my deafness. However, with gentle coaxing I had the confidence to speak out and contribute. By the end of the course I felt confident enough to see if a Cochlear Implant was still an option as I felt the time was right. After a successful operation in late 2005 I can now hear for the very first time in my life.

In May 2006 I trained for and ran in the Great Manchester run; raised £4,500 for The Ear Trust so others can benefit from Cochlear Implants and appeared on local TV, radio and featured in several local and national newspapers as well as a magazine to promote this charity. I was proud to be nominated for the Yorkshire Women of Achievement Award in May 2006 and shortlisted for the Jane Tomlinson Award for women of courage.

Another personal achievement was driving up to Northumberland alone and finding perfect accommodation. I enjoyed long walks on the beach and felt a fantastic achievement to have the independence to enjoy meals in restaurants and communicating with others. I cannot describe my new found experience. I've never enjoyed my life so much as I do now and my children are happy. I still look out for new ventures and am building new dreams.

Learnings

- identify and source the support for what you need
- make use of your support networks (family, friends, colleagues, etc.)
- set achievable goals and make them happen!

7

The Assertive You

Objective	• to equip you with knowledge and understanding of assertiveness
	• to build your confidence and skills in being assertive

This chapter is important because

- assertiveness enables you to deal with difficult situations and makes communication more effective
- there are lots of misunderstandings about assertiveness
- you need to decide for yourself which situations you want to work on by behaving assertively so that:
  - your self-confidence increases
  - you work out and achieve your goals
  - you are properly understood
  - other people know exactly where they are with you
  - you are more open to receiving feedback
  - your relationships are based on reality rather than illusion
  - you stand a better chance of getting what you want
  - you feel better for expressing your feelings
  - you succeed with more difficult situations
  - you have fewer situations that are unresolved
  - even if you do not resolve a situation, you feel better for having spoken up

Contents
- what assertiveness is and is not
- fight/flight syndrome
- assertiveness in practice
- your assertiveness agenda
- how to be assertive
- how to get better at the ingredients
- finding the right words
- tone of voice and body language
- summary and action
- profile of Tina Henderson

What assertiveness is and is not

There is a spectrum of behaviour. We are all capable of behaving aggressively, passively and assertively.

Aggressive   Passive

Aggressive behaviour is

- getting your own way, no matter what
- getting your own point across at other people's expense
- getting people to do things they don't want to do
- being loud and violent
- interrupting others
- winning at all costs

Not all aggressive behaviour is obvious or direct. There is also indirect or passive aggressive behaviour which can be:
- conveyed in a polite way
- quiet and apparently inoffensive
- manipulating or tricking people
- ignoring people

- being silent or sulking
- using sarcasm
- putting people down, making them feel small
- inoffensive on the surface

Most people have a tendency towards one form of behaviour rather than another, and vary their behaviour depending on the situation and their feelings at the time.

Aggressive behaviour doesn't come from being over-confident – quite the reverse; it comes from lack of confidence and fear. Underneath the blustery bully is a coward. It may be difficult to believe, but the person who's having a go at you is a real person underneath, who's feeling just as scared or threatened as a person behaving passively.

Passive behaviour is

- keeping quiet for fear of upsetting people
- avoiding conflict
- saying yes when you want to say no
- always putting other people's needs first
- not expressing your feelings
- going along with things you don't like or agree with
- apologising excessively
- inwardly burning with anger and frustration
- being vague about your ideas and what you want
- justifying your actions to other people
- appearing indecisive

Ever found yourself doing any of this? Many women find themselves using passive behaviour quite a lot. If so, you may have reached the point where you don't know what your views or feelings on a topic are, but somehow you have a vague feeling of dissatisfaction at being taken for granted, or not taken seriously.

Passive behaviour stems from lack of confidence. Turning passive behaviour into assertive behaviour will gradually build your confidence.

 Assertiveness is about building your own self-respect and respecting other people.

Assertive behaviour is

- being open and honest with yourself and other people
- listening to other people's points of view
- showing understanding of other people's situations
- expressing your ideas clearly, but not at the expense of others
- being able to reach workable solutions to difficulties
- making decisions – even if your decision is to not make a decision!
- being clear about your point and not being sidetracked
- dealing with conflict
- having self-respect and respect for other people
- being equal with others whilst retaining your uniqueness
- expressing feelings honestly and with care

How often are you truly assertive by these standards? Most people find they can be assertive in some types of situations but tend to be aggressive or passive in others.

Think about situations at home and at work and judge for yourself where your behaviour tends to be on the assertiveness spectrum.

Mark where you are now and then put an arrow to where you would like to be in the future.

Add any other general situations in which you know you are not as assertive as you would like to be.

BEHAVIOUR	Passive	Assertive	Aggressive
At home			
At work			
With friends			
In shops			
At the doctor's			

If people say that you are very assertive it probably means that you are generally tending to be aggressive and they are too polite or behaving too passively to tell you the truth!

Fight/flight syndrome

The fight/flight syndrome may explain your response to difficult situations.

Our bodies have evolved to help us deal with physical danger when we are faced with a difficult situation. They instinctively respond by putting us into a physically alert state (i.e. heart pounding, adrenaline flowing) which enables us to either fight the danger or run away.

Despite changes in society our instinctive physical response to difficult situations is still either to fight (aggressive behaviour) or run away (passive behaviour).

While fighting or running away might have been good tactics in the Stone Age they aren't necessarily the most effective way to deal with situations in the 21st Century. However, it does explain why people don't seem to need courses on aggressive or passive behaviour – it just comes naturally!

Remember that the root cause of aggressive and passive behaviour is fear or lack of self-confidence. So most of us are capable of swinging dramatically from one end of the scale to the other, for seemingly trivial reasons.

However, recent research indicates that fight/flight may relate more to men. Women are more likely to 'tend and befriend' so will tidy up workspaces, make things better and will then seek the company of women friends.

Throughout this workbook we use this definition of assertiveness:

Assertiveness is a form of behaviour which demonstrates your self-respect and respect for others. Assertiveness is also concerned with dealing with your own feelings about yourself and other people, as much as with the end result.

If your self-respect isn't very high then it may be difficult for you to assert yourself at the moment and your behaviour will tend to be passive; conversely, if you tend not to respect others you will tend to aggressive behaviour. Only you can truly decide what is assertive for you because only you know what you are thinking and feeling inside.

Assertiveness is about dealing with your feelings.

Assertiveness in practice

Does assertiveness always work? It depends on your objectives. It doesn't guarantee a particular outcome but if the process is followed it usually makes you feel that speaking up for yourself and expressing your feelings is worthwhile.

Your boss asks you to stay late to finish a piece of work and you are perfectly assertive in your refusal to stay. Your boss isn't in the least impressed and still insists, despite your explanation. Ultimately, she still insists and, unless you feel like resigning over it, you realise that you will have to stay late. Your assertiveness hasn't affected the outcome – you still stay late.

However, behaving assertively in that situation has helped in a number of ways:

- You preserve your self-esteem: 'At least I said what I felt and explained properly without getting upset.'
- No one can ever say that you meekly agreed: 'You never said anything last time.'
- You may have provoked your boss into re-assessing you: 'I didn't realise she felt so strongly about that, she's got more to her than I thought.'

Assertiveness may not always be practical if the other person is being very unreasonable or showing erratic behaviour e.g. dealing with a drunk.

For the rest of this chapter and the next you will be looking at developing your assertive behaviour in a way that feels appropriate to you. It doesn't mean turning shy people into raving extroverts and it doesn't mean turning zany, fun people into boring grey clones.

Your assertiveness agenda

The exercises that follow are to enable you to be really specific about your agenda for assertiveness.

Write down the real situations that you encounter, either at work or at home, where you would like to be more assertive. Start off with one that isn't very challenging at all. You could probably deal with it if you just got on with it:

Go to the other extreme, and think of the most difficult or frightening situation that you encounter, or that you are avoiding. It may be something that makes you feel quite ill to think about, and you may think that nothing can be done about it. Write it down, all the same:

Specific situations

In the next exercise you will be asked to write down more specific situations in which you want to become more assertive. Here are some examples of the types of situations other women have chosen to work on. They are not in any order of difficulty because what may be easy for one woman may be the most difficult for another, and the other way round. They are given purely as prompts to help you think of your own situations. Cover them up if you don't want to be prompted.

Personal

- dealing with comments about living alone
- stopping unwanted emails or text messages
- stopping my elderly mother from going out half-dressed
- telling my friend I only want her to stay for a week and not blaming anyone else for asking her to go
- asking my family to tidy up after themselves without nagging or getting angry
- dealing with a racist comment on the bus
- getting the children to settle for clothes that aren't 'designer'
- putting my needs first for once
- getting my mortgage/overdraft increased
- telling my partner how I feel about his/her abusiveness
- having some time to myself each day/week
- talking to my landlord about getting repairs done

Work

- working hours interfering with home life
- saying no to requests for help when I'm overloaded
- colleagues not taking turns to make tea
- refusing to help Joyce out again with her schedules
- speaking up at meetings
- standing up for what I believe in with more senior people
- persuading my boss to let me do some of her work
- dealing with a colleague who I know is lying to me
- being sexually or racially harassed at work
- being asked at an interview why I should get the job

YOUR ASSERTIVENESS AGENDA

On page 150 you wrote down an easy and a very difficult situation in which you want to be more assertive.

Now write in the easy one at No. 1 and the difficult one at No. 10 on the list below. Think of other situations to add. Make the low numbers the easier situations and the high numbers the more difficult ones.

Think of as many different situations as you can. Try to get a mixture of: home/work, friends/relatives, big/little, short term/long term situations – use the prompt sheet on the previous page if you need more ideas.

Next to each one write down how you deal with them now (passively, aggressively, indirectly aggressively).

1.

2.

3.

4.

5.

6.

7.

8.

9.

10.

 Assertiveness enables each of us to be more ourselves.

Building up notches

Every time you ignore a situation or choose not to deal with it and feel bad about it, it builds up a 'notch' of anger and resentment inside. Eventually, you can get to the point where you blow up.

Ever had days when everything seems to go wrong? Su Lin copes with this by keeping her head down and keeping out of everyone's way. She may have days, months or even years like this, going home with resentment and frustration, until something snaps. She then swings into her aggressive mode. She may lose her temper over something quite trivial, and everyone is astounded, because she's never said anything before!

How do you feel immediately after you blow up?

And how do you feel a bit later?

Most people feel great at the time and then guilty or ashamed not long after. The danger is that if you feel so guilty later that you feel bad about yourself, you may decide to keep quiet, and build up more notches; you then find yourself in a vicious circle of passive and aggressive behaviour.

Don't forget you can allow yourself NOT to be assertive too! If you know you can choose to be assertive, you can equally choose NOT to assert yourself on any occasion. You may just not feel up to it that day, or you may decide it's not appropriate. You may still choose sometimes to be aggressive or passive because it seems the best short-term solution, but generally these behaviours won't build good long-term relationships.

How to be assertive

There are no set phrases, trick techniques, or magic words in assertiveness. There are five vital ingredients in any assertive process.

1. Listen

2. Demonstrate understanding

3. Say what you think and feel

4. Say specifically what you want to happen

5. Work out joint solutions

How are you doing?

If you're still not sure whether you're behaving assertively or not, check your feelings about yourself and the other person. Remember that assertiveness is about feeling good about yourself. A useful shorthand way of looking at this is as follows:

ASSERTIVE	AGGRESSIVE
I'm OK	I'm OK
You're OK	You're not OK

PASSIVE	DEPRESSIVE
I'm not OK	I'm not OK
You're OK	You're not OK

Adapted from Thomas Harris's book, *I'm OK, You're OK* published by Pan.

How to get better at the ingredients

Being more assertive means getting better at all the ingredients and being able to move from one to the other as needed in a conversation. Here are a few hints and tips to polish up each ingredient:

1 Listen

People who are successful at being assertive are good listeners. You may be able to listen well in some circumstances but listening gets more difficult the more complex or controversial the subject matter is. Assertiveness is often about ironing out tricky situations, so listening is a key skill.

Listening is the first key ingredient in an assertive conversation. There is little hope of starting your part of the conversation by demonstrating your understanding if you haven't really taken in what is being said.

It is very difficult to listen to everything that someone is saying, particularly if:
- the other person is waffling
- you disagree with it
- the other person is expressing very strong feelings
- you experience the other's behaviour as aggressive
- there are distractions
- your mind wanders to other things
- you are busy thinking about what you are going to say

Mostly, we can spot when someone isn't listening to us.

What are the signs that you notice when someone switches off?

How do you feel when you're not being listened to?

Not being listened to tends to create negative feelings. Keep your listening active to stop these feelings building up.

People can usually spot if you are not listening to them.

Active listening

Listening well to someone takes a special active effort. It involves:

- quietening yourself down inside
- keeping distractions to a minimum
- paying attention even when you disagree or have strong feelings
- asking questions for clarification
- being open to hear the other person's thoughts, ideas, feelings and intentions
- demonstrating, as well as saying, that you have understood
- giving someone else the space to speak
- being objective about dealing with what you hear

Practise active listening.

2 Demonstrate understanding

Have you experienced someone saying to you – 'I understand how you feel, however...' and you are quite certain they **don't** understand? True assertiveness is not a set of trick phrases! In true assertiveness you need to demonstrate, by how you listen and by what you say, that you really have understood.

Put yourself in the other person's shoes and then summarise by telling them how you think they are feeling, what you think they are thinking or what it is that you think they want to do next. This gives them the opportunity to correct you if you are close but not close enough in your assessment.

Or you can relate to a similar situation you have faced.

Anne:

I had been unable to work for over two years because of a real crisis in my health when in the post one day Patricia sent me this quote and said she thought of me when she saw it.

'A long time ago, before I began my search for ways to feel better about myself, I was in a very low state. I was in the middle of a severe personal trauma and I had no self-belief. In fact I had no belief in anything. When we are in the depths of despair and suffer from low self-esteem we lose all sense of trust in ourselves and in other people, and so we feel lonely, vulnerable and afraid. This feeling of vulnerability can make us feel exposed and unprotected and very sensitive to others.'

Then I knew that she really understood how I was.

3 Say what you think and feel

Know what you think and identify your feelings, then make choices about how you communicate your thoughts and feelings.

Different cultures have different ways of communicating and even within the UK culture there is a spectrum of difference. Think back to your upbringing and the family or people that surrounded you then. How did they communicate? Was it thoughts only and not feelings? Was it through direct communication e.g. 'I feel really angry when you keep ignoring me' or indirect e.g. 'You don't seem interested in what I am saying.'

Some families, or if you were brought up in care, institutions, have a culture of never saying what they feel to each other and so your anger, hurt, guilt and sadness can go on for years without anyone ever really being clear about how you feel. Equally you may shout, scream, bang doors and throw a tantrum but still be leaving the other person to guess what it is that you are really feeling. How do they know whether your banging the door is a result of hurt, anger or whatever?

If there is no direct communication of the feelings, the other person is left to guess or has to check what you are feeling by demonstrating that she understands. Indirect communication needs to be followed up with more conversation to reach a point where you can both be sure that you understand.

When you want to say what you think and feel you can choose a direct or indirect route.

4 Say specifically what you want to happen

Dropping hints doesn't always work! Being clear about what you want to happen increases the possibility of getting it and minimises the chances of being misunderstood. Of course it doesn't guarantee that you get what you want; you have to be prepared for the other person to say no or have a different point of view. Listen to the response you get.

Judge the circumstances around your request. Have an eye on your long-term goal. If you ask for your maximum then you have room to negotiate and reach a long-term solution.

So, if your regular babysitter is telling you that she doesn't want to babysit any more you might say that you are prepared to do something special for her over the next month to encourage her to stay.

5 Work out joint solutions and the consequences

Where there is a gap between what you want and what others want, you need to work out a joint solution. A joint solution means joint problem solving to reach a solution that pleases all parties, not a compromise. Compromise means that neither of you gets what you want. In exploring joint solutions consider the consequences of each choice on yourself and the others concerned.

This is where the real understanding and negotiation starts. You only get to this stage if you have not reached agreement by using the other ingredients. All the other four ingredients need to be used time and time again to arrive at a point where you can either see the other person's point of view or they can see yours and one of you changes your point of view on what you want. If this doesn't happen then you have to agree that you cannot agree.

That's the theory and to put it into practice begin with finding the right words.

Finding the right words

Assertive behaviour involves demonstrating understanding, saying what you think and feel, saying specifically what you want to happen, and working out joint solutions. This means finding the right words.

There is masses of recent research on language that can help show differences in how men and women communicate. See the booklist in Chapter 14.

The use of words gives clues about the behaviour.

You are having trouble getting started on a piece of work which is usually routine. You say to a passing colleague:

Passive: 'Silly me, I'm getting nowhere with this. My brain must be going.'

Aggressive: 'I don't know whose stupid idea it was to say this had to be done this way. I always said this company was run by idiots!'

Assertive: 'Tracy, I know you're too busy right now, but I'm feeling really stuck on this and could do with some help. When can you spare me 10 minutes today?'

So let's concentrate on the assertive words!

Using words assertively – beginnings

Very often you have to initiate a conversation. In these cases, you can't initially listen as nothing has been said! Your opening remarks still need to:

- demonstrate that you understand
- say what you think and feel
- say specifically what you want to happen

Write down an assertive approach to these situations:

You regularly come up with good information for your boss's boss. Your boss has just rewritten your list in his/her handwriting and pretended it is his/her own. You're very upset about this. You say to her/him:

A colleague has volunteered your help to a department which is overstretched. You are already very busy and are furious that your colleague should make an assumption. You say to your colleague:

Your partner/friend rings or texts you on your mobile so frequently you think it is excessive. You say:

Now try one of your own situations from page 152 here.
Your situation:

Your beginning:

Using words assertively – replying

On other occasions you have to respond to someone else. You will need to listen and then:

- demonstrate that you understand
- say what you think and feel
- say specifically what you want to happen

Using the ingredients, write down an assertive response to these scenarios:

You are doing some DIY at home with a friend when you make a mistake. Your friend loses her/his temper and starts swearing at you and blaming you for other mistakes that have been made. You say to your friend:

You are keen to take on a new piece of work which will widen your experience and involve you staying later in the evening. Although you have volunteered for the work, your manager says: 'Well of course you won't be able to cope with this because you have to get home to look after your kids/mother/dog'. You reply:

You are applying for a job three grades above your current one and ask your manager to support your application. She/he laughs and says 'What on earth are you doing applying for that?' You reply:

Try to avoid using set phrases. Build up some new choices for assertive replies to situations that bother you. Try out one of your own situations from page 152.
Your situation:

Your reply:

Tone of voice and body language

Assertive words need to be matched by the tone of voice and body language. The communication researcher, Professor Albert Mehrabian, discovered that the messages that people receive about other people consist of these ingredients:

His research was mainly around situations where communication was ambiguous: where the words spoken are inconsistent with the tone of voice or body language of the speaker. If you are surprised or unconvinced by these statistics, consider the huge number of ways you can convey different meanings with a single word, such as 'really', just by changing the volume, pitch, speed and emphasis of your voice. So it is hardly surprising that the voice itself is more than five times more important than the words being spoken. For example: sarcasm only works if the message sent out by the voice and body overrule the actual words being said.

Words, voice, and appearance need to deliver the same message. So it's vital to match the body language and tone with the verbal message.

Think about what you hear around you and compile your own examples of aggressive, passive and assertive uses of voice:

Aggressive   **Assertive**   **Passive**

If someone is having a conversation with you on the phone, they will have to base their judgement of your message purely on your words and voice. If it is an email they have only the words and the layout of the message e.g. using capitals which equates to shouting.

Body language varies from country to country, depending on the culture, so body language has to be read in conjunction with the other signals. It is dangerous to make judgements from one gesture alone. For example, folding arms may be seen as a shutting off, aggressive gesture. It may also be that the person is cold!

We are all experts in body language. Consciously and unconsciously we read it all day. We know when someone is putting out a mixed message, when the words don't agree with the body language.

OBSERVE – How people sit in the bus, in waiting rooms, at work, and speculate on what you would read from their posture.

TRY OUT – The next time you are with a group of people, sit in a way that you think is assertive for a while – see how it feels and if it matches your words.

Body space

Another aspect of body language concerns the space we give ourselves and others.

Imagine you are travelling home late at night on a train. You are the only person in the carriage until one other passenger boards and sits right next to you, without saying a word or being threatening in any way. How do you feel?

Most of us feel extremely nervous and frightened in that situation. The stranger has become aggressive simply by invading our own personal space.

In day-to-day terms we feel comfortable with some people really close to us and with others we would rather they kept their distance. In his book

Body Language, Allan Pease describes these spaces as zones. These zones are 'portable air bubbles' that we each have around us.

Zone distances

The sizes of the zones are determined by the culture we've grown up in. For example, while some people are comfortable with crowding, other people are used to wide open spaces and prefer to keep their distance.

The radius of the air bubble around us can be broken down into four distinct zone distances:

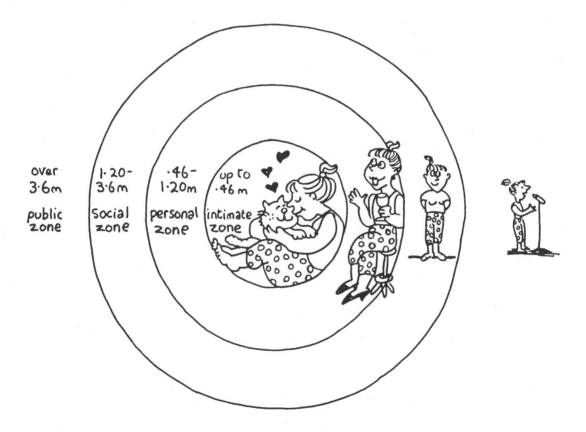

These zone distances tend to apply to people brought up in Australia, New Zealand, the UK, North America and Canada.

Intimate Zone 15 – 45cm (6 – 18in)

Of all the zone distances this is by far the most important as it is this zone that a person guards as if it were her own property. Only those who are emotionally close to that person are permitted to enter it. This includes lovers, parents, partner, children, close friends and relatives. There is also a sub-zone that extends up to 15 centimetres (6 inches) from the body which implies physical contact. This is the close intimate zone.

Personal Zone 46cm – 1.22m (18 – 48in)

This is the distance that we stand from others at parties, social functions and friendly gatherings.

Social Zone 1.22 – 3.6m (4 – 12ft)

We stand at this distance from strangers, the plumber or carpenter doing repairs, the courier, the shopkeeper, new employees at work and other people we don't know very well.

Public Zone over 3.6m (12ft)

Whenever we address a large group of people, this is the comfortable distance at which we choose to stand.

Being aware of the zones doesn't mean moving around with a tape measure around your waist, but simply being more aware of the effect of distance.

You may feel that some people stand too close to you – or don't come close enough! You may have found yourself edging down the corridor because the person you are talking to keeps coming too close, or going up close to some people and seeing them backing off.

People coming too close to you or touching you in an unwelcome way may constitute harassment. Find out if your employer has a harassment policy and decide what you want to do about it.

If you wish people to react to you in a friendly, open way, then be sensitive to the possibility of invading their space – your behaviour may be perceived as aggressive and threatening.

OBSERVE – How close do you stand to other people? Is it comfortable for you? How do you think it is for them? Make notes here about any changes you would like to make:

> **'** *Interesting how easily men own the space around them, while women just feel like visitors without a permit.* **'**

Sarah Dunant – *Fatlands*

MEDITATION – VISUALISE THE GAP

Follow your usual process of relaxing and allowing yourself to let go of today's tensions.

Now picture a person with whom you have an issue and wish to assert yourself. Imagine that person listening to you as you explain your thoughts, feelings and wishes on the issue. Hear what she or he replies and, for the moment, do not attempt to take the issue forward to resolution; simply allow yourself to be there quietly with your view and her or his view.

Stay with both positions and picture on a scale of 10 parts how far apart you seem to be on the issue. Visualise the scale and then see the points where each of you is now moving closer together.

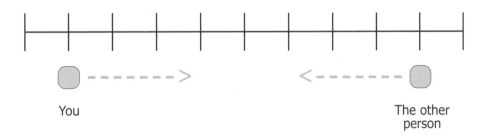

You   The other
                                       person

Return to the present time, open your eyes and focus on whatever is straight ahead of you for a few seconds.

HAVE A GO!

Turn back to page 152 and your own list of real situations.

Have a go at using assertiveness. Start by tackling your No. 1. If there isn't an appropriate moment for it then pick any of your lower numbered situations – start small:

- have a go at something which doesn't matter too much to you
- recap the main points on page 154 and see how you get on
- review your use of the five ingredient process
- record what happens below:

Situation:

I intended to:

What actually happened was:

Looking back, one thing I would do differently is:

Looking back, one thing I'm proud of is:

My feelings about the way I handled it are:

OPTIONAL ACTIVITY – PRACTISE WITH FRIENDS OR COLLEAGUES

One way to build up your skills is to practise with other people who are familiar with this way of working with assertiveness. Team up with someone who is willing to work with the five ingredients, practise acting out the situations and give each other feedback.

Summary and action

In this chapter, you have clarified the definition and learned the ingredients of assertiveness. You have practised some assertive responses and beginnings to situations. You have also prioritised situations in which you wish to be more assertive.

Further optional reading

Deborah Tannen – *You just don't understand* – published by Virago
Trades Union Congress – *Sexual Harassment at Work* – published by the TUC
Allan Pease – *Body Language* – published by Sheldon Press
Allan and Barbara Pease – *Why men don't listen and women can't read maps* – published by Sheldon Press

Action

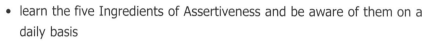

What actions will you take now to be more assertive?

- learn the five Ingredients of Assertiveness and be aware of them on a daily basis
- practise saying no when you mean no
- get feedback from people close to you about how you come across; share the definitions first because sometimes people tell a woman that she is very assertive when she is actually behaving aggressively!
- celebrate the success you've had with your own situations
- decide which of your own assertiveness situations you will deal with next and jot them down here

Write yours here:

Specific Action   **By When?**

Profile *Tina Henderson*

Job Title: Watch Manager
Organisation: Suffolk Fire & Rescue Service

Who am I? Good question. To begin with, I have achieved a happy and worthwhile promotion in a working environment predominantly made up of men – I am a Watch Manager in the Fire Service. But more importantly 'who am I' – a working single mum to two adorable children who make everything worthwhile.

Mine is not a story of heroes, it's a tale of a normal woman who strongly believes that she's responsible for making her own choices in life. Whether they lead to happier times is yet to be seen, but I have no regrets and it's a great feeling. I have spent the past six years working in the Fire Service. I began as a firefighter who achieved the Silver Axe for top recruit, a feat never achieved by a female in our brigade before. Did I get recognition? No! The rumours circulated that 'it's only because she's a woman'. Well actually it was because I was extremely good at my job – something I have always been proud of.

During my first year of this exciting and demanding career my marriage fell apart with the most hurtful words... 'You are turning into a man'. My hair was short, my nails broke – it's hard work saving people for a living. I did what many women would do upon hearing this, I grew my hair and had monthly false nail manicures – anything to save my doomed marriage. But to no avail.

So my first decision. Do I continue in a profession when everything feels like an uphill struggle at times? The answer was a resounding 'yes'. I was doing this for me and I felt very comfortable with this choice. I am a firm believer that my children can't be happy until I'm happy, and a career in the Fire Service is what I wanted and deserved. I would like to say it's been easy and I've sailed through so far, but that isn't true. Most weeks I come across the amazed, glazed look of 'how can a woman be in this profession?' Mostly, it has to be said, from the public. 'Surely you don't ride the fire engine; you must just make the tea?!' Well no, I do everything a man does and more...

So where am I now? My brigade asked me to run a national recruitment campaign in the hope of not only recruiting promising capable individuals but of also attracting the attention of our under represented groups – females and ethnic minorities. I embraced this new challenge and far exceeded even my hopes of it being a success. We had the largest ever response from these under represented groups and have increased our numbers by 20% in both areas. A fantastic achievement which I am very proud of.

But my biggest achievement so far is bringing up and setting examples for my children to help them grow into responsible, well-adjusted and, more importantly, happy adults. I am a very hands-on mum with my two children. My little boy, who is eight, is proving to have a strong talent for football so I currently take him to necessary training three times a week. My daughter, turning 13, is fascinated with how I do my makeup – so normally I have her stuck at my side when I'm applying mine just to see how I put eye liner on straight and how I don't poke my eye out with my mascara.

As for me, I love to socialise and catch up with my friends at every opportunity, normally this is at aqua aerobics which is where we tend to chat and giggle about what has happened to us all during the week. I also have a one and a half year old staffy (Staffordshire Bull Terrier) dog – as a family we enjoy walking him at weekends. I love the sun, so normally attempt to take me and the children abroad each year. As a single parent family we have been to Cuba, Egypt, Lanzarote and Cyprus.

My children know that everyone is responsible for their own choices in life no matter which path they may choose or what obstacles are in their way. I'm not one of life's victims and I never intend to be.

Learnings

- make it your priority if something is important to you
- be true to yourself
- be proud of your achievements – big or small
- don't let people pin labels on you

> *This above all: to thine own self be true*
> *And it must follow, as the night the day,*
> *Thou canst not then be false to any man. (or woman!)*
>
> Shakespeare – *Hamlet*

Using Assertiveness Positively

Objective
- to put assertiveness skills into practice to help you achieve your goals

This chapter is important because

- assertiveness is easy in theory, but difficult in practice
- the basic ingredients can be adapted to fit different circumstances

Contents
- practising assertiveness
- using assertiveness when you:
  - are asked for straight information
  - find inconsistency in someone's behaviour
  - need a response from someone
  - aren't being listened to, or aren't being taken notice of
  - are dealing with someone's strong feelings
  - have strong feelings yourself
  - want to say no
  - give and receive criticism
  - give or receive a compliment
- being assertive with yourself
- summary and action
- profile of Judith Secker

Practising assertiveness

In this chapter you have the opportunity to see how you can find the words to be assertive in a wide range of different situations.

Using assertiveness when you are asked for straight information

It hardly seems necessary to learn assertiveness in order to reply to a straight question, but many people tie themselves in verbal knots to avoid giving straight answers to straight questions.

For example

'What time is the meeting on Tuesday?'

Passive: 'Umm – I think it might be 3 o'clock, but then I'm not sure. You'd better check with someone else. Sorry.'

Aggressive: 'You mean you don't know? You were there when it was organised. Why don't you get yourself together?'

Assertive: '3 o'clock.'

YOUR ASSERTIVE REPLIES

Write down your assertive reply to these questions:

'Who's going to make the tea?'

'When will you have that report ready for me?'

'How do you feel about this Springboard Workbook right now?'

Using assertiveness when you find inconsistency in someone's behaviour

An inconsistency may be:
- when someone says one thing and does another
- when someone contradicts something they've already said
- when the printed policy says one thing and the accepted practice is another
- when someone says one thing and looks as if they mean another

The assertive response is not to demand that everything is consistent in life, but to:
- point out the inconsistency
- express the effect of the inconsistency on you
- say what you want to happen

For example

'You said I didn't have enough experience so I didn't apply for the promotion. Now it's been given to someone with less experience than me. I'm very confused and annoyed about this, and I would like an explanation.'

YOUR ASSERTIVE RESPONSE

Write an assertive response to these inconsistencies:

Your partner has been extremely supportive of you and your career, but has recently started making sarcastic remarks when you work on your revision for your exams.

At your manager's suggestion, you have organised a day out to visit other parts of your current organisation and are keen to go. Your manager now says you can't go because of work pressure.

Using assertiveness when you need a response from someone

When someone uses passive behaviour, it can be difficult to discover what their thoughts and feelings are. They may not know what they are or have decided it is not relevant or appropriate, or be too scared to express them.

Alternatively, someone may be indirectly aggressive and be choosing not to speak. You may prefer them to voice their opinion on a subject at the time, so you know where you stand and can avoid them saying afterwards: 'Well of course, I never actually agreed with that decision.'

The assertive approach is to make very specific requests to individuals.

For example

'Well, we've aired the subject of the new computers at length. I'm pretty clear about where Gina, Tom and Andrea stand. Des, I'd like to hear your views on this.'

YOUR ASSERTIVE RESPONSE

Write down how you would find out:

How your partner feels about going to your family again for Christmas, Divali, Eid or some other special time?

What's wrong with a friend who has been very quiet since you were promoted to a grade higher?

Using assertiveness when you aren't being listened to, or aren't being taken notice of

When you suspect you aren't being listened to the tendency is to move towards either aggressive or passive behaviour. An assertive way of dealing with this is simply to repeat the essential parts of your message, while continuing to acknowledge the other person.

For example

Your Manager and you are about to go to a meeting and she/he is hassling you to get to the meeting on time.

Manager: 'Come on, we'll be late for the meeting.'
You: 'We've got 10 minutes yet, I'll be ready.'
Manager: 'We'd better get going now.'
You: 'I'll be ready within 10 minutes.'

MAKING SURE YOU'RE HEARD

Work out an assertive way of ensuring that you are heard in these situations:

You are at a meeting where it is assumed that you will stay until 6 pm. You need to leave at 5pm to collect your children from the childminder.

You are explaining to your friend that you do not want her to assume that you will always go out with her on Thursday nights.

Using assertiveness when you are dealing with someone's strong feelings

One of the vital ingredients in assertiveness is to demonstrate your understanding of the other person. When you think that a situation is particularly sensitive, and feelings are running strongly, it is even more important to demonstrate your understanding. This doesn't mean you have to agree with the other person, but demonstrating your understanding keeps communication going.

Anger is for many the most difficult emotion to deal with. When people are very angry they often don't say 'I'm very angry' or 'I'm furious', but it is obvious from their tone and appearance. Acknowledging the feeling often diffuses it.

For example

You think your mother is angry about something because she keeps snapping at you.

You: 'You seem angry or upset. What's the matter?'

YOUR ASSERTIVE RESPONSE

A colleague has just returned to work after having arranged her father's funeral. Acknowledge what's happened:

A neighbour shouts at you because he thinks you were playing loud music late at night and kept him awake. It wasn't you. Acknowledge his feelings and resolve the situation:

Using assertiveness when you have strong feelings yourself

It isn't always possible to think of something positive to say in every situation. Sometimes all you're left with are negative feelings and wishing things were different. In these circumstances, say so. It is important to:

- be very specific
- describe the behaviour that you find upsetting, rather than having a go at the person
- say how this affects you
- say what you would like to happen next

For example

'When you drive this close to the car in front, I feel very nervous. Could you leave a bit more space?'

EXPRESS YOUR FEELINGS ASSERTIVELY

Write down your response, saying how you feel and what you would like to happen:

Your friend is flicking through magazines and saying 'mmmm' while you're trying to say something really important to her.

You have been working very hard to organise a staff meeting on childcare facilities, which you are very keen to attend. Your boss now tells you that she thinks there is no reason for you to attend the meeting and wants you to answer the phones while everyone else goes.

Using assertiveness when you want to say 'no'

'No' is one of the shortest but most difficult words for most of us to say.

Write down why you have difficulty saying 'no':

No wonder saying 'yes' is easier, even when you'd prefer to say 'no'!

Assertive behaviour means saying 'no' and backing it up with an explanation if you wish. It does not mean making excuses or apologies or justifying yourself, i.e. going on and on giving excuses (sometimes not even true ones!) so that the other person will think well of you or at least think your reasons are good enough.

For example

'Could you give me a lift to the station?'

Passive: 'I'm sorry – I can't. I would if I could, but tonight I've got to be at the other end of town to pick my sister up, and the traffic might be bad and I don't want to upset her by being late again. I'm ever so sorry.'

Aggressive: 'Not likely. No way. Why should I?'

Assertive: 'No' plus an assertive explanation if you wish, e.g. 'No, I'm picking my sister up tonight.'

OBSERVE HOW PEOPLE SAY 'NO'

Over the next two days listen to yourself and other people saying 'no' and make notes on how people do it well.

Using assertiveness when you need to give criticism

As with saying 'no', many people avoid criticism as it can be uncomfortable and negative. Giving criticism assertively gives opportunities for change to happen, and often clears the air.

There are five steps in giving criticism assertively:

1. *Give specific examples of the behaviour you're criticising*

2. *Say how you feel about the effect it has on you*

3. *Say what changes you'd prefer to see*

4. *Listen to the response (words, voice and body language)*

5. *Work out a joint solution (not a compromise), to take you into the future – don't get bogged down in what has happened*

For example

You overhear a colleague making a sarcastic remark about another colleague.

You: 'When you talk about Angela like that I feel really angry. I don't like the implication that she's slow on the uptake and I'd rather you didn't talk about her like that.'

GIVE SOME CRITICISM

Think of a real situation where you would like to give criticism in order to bring about a change. Write it down, then try it out:

Using assertiveness when you need to receive criticism

Remaining open to receiving criticism takes courage. It is one of the ways you have of finding out the effect you have on other people and enables you to decide whether you want to change your behaviour or not. Do not fall into the trap of feeling you have to justify yourself.

There are four steps:

> *Remain open – listen to what is being said and ask for specific examples to clarify your own understanding*
>
> *Let the other person know you've heard and understood the criticism, by giving the other person your immediate response*
>
> *Take time to decide: is it all true, is it partly true, is it totally false, what do you want to do?*
>
> *Change your behaviour if you want to*

For example

'I can see that my not speaking up at meetings could be interpreted as my not being interested. I'm not sure how I feel about that at the moment, and will give it some thought.'

PRACTISE 'CRITICISM SITUATIONS'

If you are working through this workbook with other women, get together with two of them to practise giving and receiving criticism, and to do the exercise on the next page. If you are working through it on your own, see who among your family/friends/colleagues will be prepared to read the sections on assertiveness and join you in practising:

1. Person One describes the scene and the characters briefly and in the practice asserts herself.

2. Person Two plays the other person, behaving as briefed by Person One.

3. If there is a third person, ask them to observe the practice and be ready to give feedback.

4. After the practice, participants and observers discuss what they have seen and heard and make constructive suggestions. You may then want to have another go.

Practise:
- giving criticism
- receiving criticism
- observing and giving feedback

Make a note of what you learnt, and have a go at compliments.

 Being open to criticism enables you to grow.

Using assertiveness when you need to give or receive a compliment

We live in a culture where compliments are regarded with great suspicion. Giving them and receiving them is difficult, as people may either think that you're 'crawling' to them or that you have an ulterior motive. Giving and receiving feedback, including compliments, is an important aspect of assertiveness.

183

Receiving compliments well boosts your self-esteem. People with less self-esteem tend to discount all compliments. Make sure you listen to the ones that come your way. Aim to give out compliments and positive feedback at least 20 times as often as you give criticism or negative feedback.

To give a compliment – keep it short and to the point.

To receive a compliment – keep it short and don't push it away or run yourself down. You may also want to say how you feel.

For example

Receiving a compliment:
'You made a really good job of that piece of work.'

Passive: 'Oh it wasn't particularly difficult – John did most of it anyway.'
Aggressive: (sarcastic) 'Oh you noticed, did you?'
Assertive: 'Thanks. I was pleased with it too.'

GIVING AND RECEIVING REAL COMPLIMENTS

Practise giving and receiving compliments with two friends or colleagues:
- Person One gives a real compliment to
- Person Two who listens, stays open minded and accepts it, while
- Person Three observes how the other two get on, then gives feedback

Then swap roles until everyone has had two turns in each role.

YOUR AGENDA FOR ACTION

Write down some situations in which you want to be more assertive. Choose whichever of the following categories are relevant to you:

Giving straight information

Inconsistency in someone's behaviour

Getting a response from someone

When you aren't being listened to or being taken notice of

When you are dealing with other people's strong feelings

When you have strong feelings yourself

When you want to say 'no'

When you need to give criticism

When you need to receive criticism

When you need to give or receive a compliment

Tackle three of these over the next two weeks.

MEDITATION

Close your eyes, relax your body and breathe easily and slowly. Imagine that as you breathe in you are breathing in a fine mist of a colour that you need right now to strengthen you. Choose any colour that you wish and allow the colour to change if you want it to. Use colour in a way that helps you, even if the colour generally has other meanings, e.g. blue – calm and restful, yellow – lightness and energy. You may not find blue restful! So decide your own meaning. Spend two to five minutes concentrating on this breathing.

Now imagine that as you breathe out you are also able to breathe out a colour that will help a situation that needs to be resolved in the world or in a group or community that you care about. As you breathe out imagine your breath somehow reaching that situation in a positive way. Do this for two to five minutes.

When you think you are reaching a conclusion round off your meditation by bringing your attention back into the place where you are now, open your eyes and stretch your body.

Being assertive with yourself

Difficulties with assertiveness often start before we open our mouths, as the most challenging relationship to handle is the relationship we have with ourselves. This sets the scene for our relationships with other people.

Being assertive with yourself:
- stops you underrating yourself
- identifies what you really need
- makes you more productive
- lets you know what you're good at
- helps your actions follow your intentions

The conversations we have with ourselves have a huge effect on the outcomes of situations. They usually become self-fulfilling prophecies, so if you're feeling anxious and sceptical about something, it is likely that you will only 'tune in' to those aspects which fit with your anxiety and scepticism.

In the examples that follow, if the unassertive voice is allowed to rule, the day will be a disaster and the meeting with the friend could end with a row. The assertive voice gives a much better chance of success.

UNASSERTIVE VOICE

'It's Tuesday and it's the departmental meeting. That means everyone's going to be in a bloody mood. It also means I'll be given all sorts of stupid things to do. If that Ian asks me for one more special favour I'll scream! I don't know how I'm going to get through the day.'

'I've read all the stuff on assertiveness now, and it seems pretty straightforward. I'll catch Parveen tonight and tell her that I'm not going to her party next week. I'm sure she'll see my point. I'll just give it to her straight.'

ASSERTIVE VOICE

'It's Tuesday and it's the departmental meeting – usually a difficult day. I'll deal with each situation as it crops up and practise remaining calm and assertive. I'll say 'no' to Ian if I have no time to do him a favour.'

'I'll be open and honest with Parveen tonight and discuss with her how I feel about her party next week. It won't necessarily be a comfortable conversation but it's important for me to sort it out.'

The final aspect of being assertive with yourself involves believing in your own feelings, and really valuing them. This may mean breaking away from your habitual patterns of behaviour, to really explain what's going on inside yourself, and stop making excuses to yourself:

• your assertive self is honest, rational, sane and realistic
• your assertive self is able to assess your own performance realistically

and objectively
- your assertive self encourages you
- your assertive self may get shouted down by the other voices

What do the other, non-assertive voices say, to stop you being assertive with yourself?

For example

Your sympathetic friend: 'Her needs are greater than mine.'

Your critic: 'Is that the best you can do? It's terrible.'

Your mouse: 'They'll misunderstand me – I'll just keep quiet.'

Your perfectionist: 'If you can't do it perfectly, then it's not worth even starting.'

Your moaner: 'What can I do? There's no point. Nobody will listen.'

RESPONDING TO YOUR NON-ASSERTIVE VOICES

Add some of your own and write down what you are going to say to them the next time they speak up:

Voice   **Your positive response**

YOUR ASSERTIVENESS AGENDA

Think of situations in which you are now going to be more assertive with yourself and add them to the ones on pages 152 and 184. You've already practised or dealt with some of them, so tackle another one, and work up to your No. 10. Aim to have dealt with most of them, including No. 10, by the end of the workbook.

Don't worry about getting it perfect. Have a go and assertively review your achievements.

Summary and action

In this chapter you have worked through examples of being assertive in many different situations.

YOUR PERSONAL RESOURCE BANK

On page 274, note the situations in which you now feel you can be truly assertive.

Further optional reading

Ken and Kate Back – *Assertiveness at work* – published by McGraw Hill

Action

What actions will you take now to develop your assertiveness further?

Here are some suggestions:

- tackle some of the many situations that you've noted down
- review progress and don't give up!
- get yourself on an assertiveness workshop
- practise accepting compliments well

Write yours here:

Specific Action   **By When?**

*Take care of the small steps – the big changes
will then take care of themselves.*

Profile *Judith Secker*

Job Title: Professional Development Adviser
Organisation: University of Oxford

My story starts in the mid-1970s with life as a librarian
ending when I became a trade union representative.
Naturally quiet, as a trade unionist I found my voice
through my values which are about equality – specifically
working for those who find it hardest to get their voices heard. That led to
my first career as a union official. In the 1970s and 1980s unions were a
man's world. However, by changing employers and with supportive managers
(both men and women) who were also mentors I gained promotion from my
first clerical job to a research post and finally to a negotiating role. The
example I gained from those managers has encouraged me to support and
mentor others in turn.

My marriage ended in 1981 when I left my husband for my long term partner.
For 15 years this partnership, bringing up my daughter alongside my partner's
two sons and my union work were my world. The partnership had its
problems, not least his unkindness towards me when we lost our unborn
baby. So I was sad but not surprised when he said that he wanted to split up
so that he could 'sort himself out'. A week later my world fell apart when my
identical twin sister announced that she and my partner were together. My
sister and I were born to parents who led quiet, frugal lives in a world where
married couples stayed together. My sister's betrayal damaged us all. I lost
my partner, his sons and my sister and was left supporting emotionally
bewildered parents.

This situation was beyond the wise words of my wonderful friends and getting
professional counselling was a breakthrough. Small steps helped me to slowly
recover – redecorating a room, throwing away my partner's possessions etc.
And I made some key decisions that first year. I wrote to my sister formally
severing contact and, with my daughter now at university, I began to think
about leaving London for a new start.

A year later I began my second career as equal opportunities officer at Oxford University. I'm glad that I took my great leap sideways when I did. Working for a research university is mentally demanding – and in my mid-40s rusty parts of my brain began to stir. Three years on, with the help of more great mentoring, I was promoted to become deputy head of personnel. For five years I worked long hours to keep the workload under control and my health began to suffer.

My decision to retire early and to work part-time with reduced responsibility was driven partly by my role as a Springboard trainer which reminded me that my personal values would be better served in a development rather than a management role. I also wanted more time for family. My daughter, having spent two years as a volunteer teacher in Eritrea, had married and brought her husband home to London.

Although I have faced adversity in my life I do not see myself as a victim but as having moved from one equilibrium to another. My inner strength was tested when I saw my sister for the first time in 10 years at our mother's funeral. Despite the sadness of the occasion, the support of friends and some positive 'head tapes' enabled me to maintain the necessary distance from her in ways that didn't cause unnecessary grief for others.

Now I am living in a great community, enjoying four-day weekends and learning another new trade at work. Having lost one family in devastating circumstances my daughter has brought me a new extended African family. Aged 54 I have started my third career, taking care of my work/life balance and heeding my personal values. I am also about to become a granny!

Learnings

- seek out positive support and mentoring
- pass on your support to other women
- get professional support when you need it
- take care of your work/life balance

9

> 6 *Go placidly amid the noise and haste.* 9
>
> Max Ehrmann – *Desiderata*

More Energy –
Less Anxiety

Objectives
- to recognise your levels of stress and pressure
- to develop healthy ways to deal with stress and overcome pressure
- to find ways to raise your energy level when you need to

This chapter is important because

- your energy needs to be maintained or recharged
- prevention is better than cure
- dealing with small pressures stops them becoming major stresses

Contents
- healthy pressure levels
- how do you know when you're stressed?
- making a fresh start
- practical exercises and activities
- summary and action
- profile of Anita McGeough

Balancing the conflicting demands of a busy life can become a major headache or it can be a dynamic and interesting way of living. The key to more energy and less anxiety is balance. There can be no prescriptions as each person has to find her own point of balance.

This chapter gives hints and tips for assessing your pressure levels, keeping going, making sure you don't burn out, raising your energy when you need it and remembering to have fun!

Healthy pressure levels

Pressure is healthy as long as you don't overdo it. Where the level of work and activity in your life is about right you will generally feel OK. Distress or, in some cases, disease results when:

- you're not aware of the level of pressure that you are putting your mind and body under
- you have too much or too little to do
- you don't like what you are doing
- what you have to do is too difficult, boring, time-consuming
- you keep going beyond your energy resources
- you are creating fight/flight energy and not using it up
- unexpected events and pressure overwhelm you

Physical and emotional symptoms usually creep in unnoticed until we become ill or unhappy. The best way to manage pressure levels is to notice them early.

Experiment now as you read this. Freeze your body in the position it is in right this minute. Notice where the tension is in your body, how much pressure you're putting on any one spot. Let go as much of the tension as you can and balance your body as best you can to save pressure or tension on that spot.

When you are under pressure, where do you usually feel tension in your body?

One of the toughest aspects of a BBC career is the constant demands it makes on time and energy. This is a critical issue for me, since I'm a single parent with twin daughters. It's ironic that, at a stage when I most want to be free to enjoy family life, I'm obliged to make a pretty substantial commitment to the job on which our livelihood depends.

At the same time I'm aware of the need to keep at least a little time for myself – which helps me function better at work, and enriches family life. I regularly make time to swim and take exercise; I like to play music, read books, go to the theatre; and I find space for a wide range of friends.

Caroline Adam
Commissioning Schedule Executive, BBC Scotland

What is the stress level in your life now?

over the top, too much pressure ☐
a bit high, some pressure ☐
comfortable, just right pressure ☐
uncomfortable, too little pressure ☐

What causes you stress now?

What are you already doing about it?

What do you foresee that may cause you stress in the near future?

How do you know when you're stressed?

People know they are stressed when they get ill or find themselves in distress, but what about your early warning signals?

Do you experience any of these?

one or two nights of not sleeping well	YES/NO
dropping things	YES/NO
forgetting things	YES/NO
biting nails, lip or cheek	YES/NO
diarrhoea	YES/NO
wanting more time to yourself	YES/NO
eating too much/too little	YES/NO
smoking more	YES/NO
drinking more alcohol	YES/NO
taking non-prescription drugs	YES/NO
feeling sick	YES/NO
expecting yourself to do more/better	YES/NO
being irritable	YES/NO
having minor accidents	YES/NO
feeling angry, hurt, worried, unhappy	YES/NO
having aches and pains	YES/NO
feeling tense	YES/NO
getting breathless on little exertion	YES/NO
high blood pressure	YES/NO
high cholesterol	YES/NO

Add anything of your own that you know or think is a symptom of your being stressed:

How many symptoms are you experiencing now?

Most people know a lot about how to prevent stress, but don't actually do enough to put what they know into practice. There is a mass of information on the internet and in the media that can inform you. Every week on TV there are several programmes on health, diet, exercise and wellbeing generally. Watch a few to get yourself better informed.

One simple way to alleviate stress is to try again to put into practice the things that you know or expect will help. Fresh-start days are the ones where you forgive yourself for having failed many times before and try again!

Making a fresh start

What needs most attention? Choose one or two areas to explore

	mega urgent	urgent	can wait
Diet			
Drinking water			
Smoking			
Overdoing alcohol			
Taking non-prescription drugs			
Exercise			
Pace of your life			
How full your life is			
Inner calmness or the lack of it			
Lack of fun			

Other positive strategies

Search the internet or look in your doctor's or dentist's waiting room, health food shops, complementary medical practices, your local sports centre, library or newsagent's window to find out what is availably locally.

The second key is to ask and explore. Sometimes you may meet someone who has a presence that you would like to have or who seems to be very fit and healthy. You may simply begin by asking them how they got to where they are and what they do to keep going. The answer could be a weekly aromatherapy massage or facial, a morning jog, regular coaching or counselling, a positive attitude recently acquired, a keen interest in rambling across beautiful countryside or whatever.

The final step is to use the positive nurturing part of yourself to make sure that you go and do it, whatever 'it' is, and reward yourself for doing it and keep on doing it if you enjoy it.

I found acupuncture helped me to manage pain levels caused by multiple sclerosis and increased my energy levels. I enjoyed massage of every sort as it helped to unknot muscle spasms. I spent a year going to a neurological gym and that helped me regain balance and co-ordination. I later joined a gym to continue the good work. I also found that osteopathy helped relieve me of muscle spasm and realigned my bones, helping me to co-ordinate my posture. After a few years I found a treatment called the Bowen Technique, which helped to move muscles back in place and helps me to relax. I started learning shiatsu massage I enjoyed it so much!

Dealing with the physical symptoms was one thing, but I needed to work as hard on the emotional and unconscious wellbeing too. Counselling and hypnosis helped me to educate my unconscious and build my internal resources.

Rachel Paul

Note any strategies you have tried or would like to try:

Practical exercises and activities

There are also many short exercises and techniques to help you overcome nerves. The rest of this chapter gives some ideas.

Overcoming nerves

In day-to-day activities people may experience sudden attacks of nerves, panic or anxiety. Nerves are normal and their effects can be overcome or at least minimised. So if, for example, you find yourself getting nervous before an interview, at the beginning of a talk, or in any other day-to-day home or work situation, try some of these exercises.

Each one takes only a couple of minutes. Some of them will be more appropriate to you and your circumstances than others. All of them have cumulative effects. Doing them regularly is like putting money in your calmness bank, which you can then draw on in times of need. Develop your own programme and use the chart on page 205 to keep yourself on track.

The keys to overcoming nerves are:
- breathing
- letting go
- preparation
- timing

Breathing

Breathing is automatic – thankfully. But it isn't automatically done well. Many people breathe high up in the ribcage and the abdomen doesn't move at all. This means only a small proportion of the air in your lungs is changed and your body loses the energy it might have from a richer supply of oxygen. To improve your breathing think about it, or work on it, for only a minute or two at a time. Don't go on too long or you'll get dizzy! If you've been doing the meditations earlier in the workbook you will have built up some experience.

TWO-MINUTE PAUSE

Wherever you are sitting, make yourself upright and comfortable and when you've read all the instructions, begin:

- note the time
- close your eyes or just lower them to the ground if you are somewhere too public
- breathe through your nose, concentrating on breathing out extra, pushing the air out with your tummy muscles. This is better for you than taking in a deep breath
- let your breathing settle again and repeat the longer out-breath three times
- then sit quietly just noticing the breath going in and out over your upper lip until you estimate two minutes have passed
- open your eyes and check the time

The first time you do this, two minutes may seem a long time, or it may have passed quickly. If you haven't done this kind of exercise before it may seem strange or you may feel self-conscious. Do persevere. Practise pausing regularly and you'll get better and better at it and it will calm you down more effectively.

Enhancing your breathing a few times a day balances out and counteracts the times you hold your breath or breathe too shallowly. You can also use this exercise before interviews or other nerve-wracking events.

Remember – breathe out!

Letting go

Letting go is the next step in overcoming nerves. Try three ways:

- physically
- emotionally
- mentally

Physically

Letting go can be achieved by breathing and relaxation techniques, or by exercise. Find out what suits you. If your job is too busy or involves too much travelling to allow you to attend classes, build up the two-minute pause on the previous page to relax your whole body. You can build on it by also doing:

TWO-MINUTE RELEASE

Start as for the two-minute pause then tell each part of your body to release. Say the word 'release' softly or silently. It's gentle. Repeat it slowly and quietly to yourself while you:

- release your
    - *head*
    - *face muscles*
    - *jaw and teeth*
- let your shoulders drop
- release your
    - *neck*
    - *shoulders*
    - *arms*
    - *chest*
    - *tummy*
    - *legs*
    - *feet*

Go into as much detail as you like. Remember – you may not feel anything happening at first, but keep going to build up the experience.

PALMING

Try 'palming' to let go of the tension around your eyes.

Sit at a table. Put your elbows on it and cover your closed eyes with the palms of your hands. After two minutes you'll find you relax more and your vision improves.

Emotionally

Letting go emotionally means reaching the point where your feelings calm down. Firstly, recognise the feeling – and express it, if appropriate. Use your assertive skills to help you resolve situations that trouble you. Secondly, accept the feeling rather than criticise yourself for having it. Thirdly, use the letting go exercise below.

TWO-MINUTE LETTING GO

What feeling do you want to let go of? Make a clear picture in your mind of the scene or scenes that have given rise to the feeling.

It's helpful if you can select one significant part of what happened; a look on someone's face, a phrase or noise you heard. Make the picture clearly in your mind.

Now erase the picture as you would wipe something off a board and when the thoughts and feelings well up in you again, remind yourself that you are working on it and will only think about it again in this relaxed setting.

If you feel you need to digest the situation and the feelings more, set some time aside and contain it rather than allowing the situation to invade the rest of the day.

Note any undigested feelings you'd like to work more on here:

Mentally

Letting go mentally involves controlling your mind, being in charge of the circling thoughts and inner conversations.

Thinking about a problem can be a really useful way of getting to grips with it, but when your mind starts going round and round on a problem and won't let go of it, it becomes stressful, unproductive and energy draining.

Try getting your mind under control. Why bother? Think of the time that is taken up with scattered thoughts when you need to get on with something. Good time-management means good quality thinking too. Here are three key ways to get your mind under control:
- concentration – to sharpen up your ability to focus on a situation and give it your best attention
- preparation – to size up the situation
- containment – to prevent your worry about a situation using up further time and energy

Concentration

Try this two-minute concentration exercise on something totally unimportant. If you practise it regularly every day for a month, you'll find your concentration on more important things improves enormously.

Two-minute Concentration

Take a very simple object that comes to hand such as a pen, paper clip, or teaspoon and concentrate on it for two minutes. For the two minutes think about as many aspects of the object as possible. For example:
- what it is
- where it came from
- what it looks like
- how it is made
- what it is made of
- what it is used for
- what it could be used for

When you find your mind wandering, bring it back to the object. Don't worry if at first you run out of thoughts before the two minutes are up.

Preparation

Planning substitutes thinking for worry! Having a plan and being prepared enables you to contain any worrying and to feel more in control. The main stress factor for many people is worry about the future. Work out your plan of what you want to achieve and how you will achieve it. This may lead to a string of thoughts that may begin with 'What if...', e.g. What if the train is late? What if they ask me about budgeting? What if she says 'no'? Part of your planning for an event needs to include your 'What if's'.

Think of one event in the future that you are apprehensive about. Pin down one of your 'what if' statements about this event. Then put down every idea you can come up with to deal with it, from the most reasonable to the downright crazy!

What if...   **I will...**

Containment

Containment is a way of disciplining your mind to choose what you think about. It means only allowing yourself to think, plan, review an event at the times that you choose. It means forcing your mind to think of other things when it strays onto the event at a time you haven't planned and only taking action about the event when it fits in with your plan. With self discipline and practice – it works.

You've tried lots of short exercises to help overcome nerves. Select the ones you are now going to use to build up your calmness bank over the next three weeks. Keep a record of your progress on this chart:

	Week 1	Week 2	Week 3
Mon			
Tues			
Wed			
Thurs			
Fri			
Sat			
Sun			

Timing

Choose your timing to suit you. For example, if you fret and worry when you do things at the last minute, then follow your inclination and do things well before the deadline even if other people think you're silly! Equally, if you work well under pressure, set tight deadlines.

Go with your rhythm

- **Daily** – Are you a morning or an evening person? Plan to do your difficult tasks at the best time for you. On days when you're feeling good, do the things you've been putting off.
- **Weekly** – Is there a pattern? – Are you refreshed on Mondays or do you only really get going by Wednesday?
- **Monthly** – What happens when you've worked solidly for three weeks without a day off? How does your menstrual cycle affect you? How do you cope with weekends being busy as well as weekdays?
- **Yearly** – When do you make new starts, and when do you slump? Is it January, or your birthday, or in September after the summer holidays? Which are your easiest months and which do you struggle through?

Stretch yourself by doing something when you're not quite ready

Stretch yourself – do this when you're bored or without enough to do. Too often we wait till we're pretty sure we can do something perfectly. If you always wait till you're absolutely ready, it may be too late.

In 1993 I was diagnosed with breast cancer and subsequently underwent a mastectomy. It was one of the most terrifying experiences of my life. There was no offer of support at the time and I had to actively seek my own. I had counselling, which kept me functioning sanely during this period.

When I recovered, I started a telephone helpline to support women affected by cancer, as there was no support of that kind in the geographical area where I lived. 12 years later, Positive Action on Cancer is a registered charity that offers a free professional counselling service for anyone affected by a cancer diagnosis. This includes family, friends and carers as well as cancer patients. PAC is also a bereavemant service for people who have lost a loved one to cancer, which is fast becoming a leading cancer service in the West Country. Recently two satellite services were opened in Bath and Warminster.

Jill Miller

MEDITATION

Breathe slowly and easily and allow your body to relax and release any areas of excess tension. Think about some aspect of your life that you wish to change in relation to reducing stress or looking after yourself better. Picture the end result that you would like to achieve.

If you wish to be fitter then imagine yourself the shape you want to be – see yourself undertaking some energetic activity that you enjoy or would like to enjoy. Really build up the picture in your mind's eye of you doing whatever it is that you want to do and achieving the end result that you wish. Go through all the stages of getting ready to do it, doing it and, afterwards, patting yourself on the back for having done it.

When you are finished, smile and then bring your attention back into the present. Remember – it's the act of smiling that releases the happy hormones.

Keep it in balance

Get the balance right for you. On their death beds, or in old age, people are unlikely to say 'I wish I'd spent more time doing housework' or 'I wish I'd spent more time at the office.' It's more likely to be 'I wish I'd taken more risks' or 'I wish I'd had more time with my family'.

 Remember your 'me time'. Build in some time each day to do something for yourself. It's a great de-stressor.

'I'd pick more daisies'

A final note on stress is best said by Nadine Stair from Louisville when she was 87 years old:

❛

If I had my life to live over, I'd try to make more mistakes next time. I would relax. I would limber up. I would be sillier than I have been this trip. I would be crazier. I would be less hygienic. I would take more chances. I would take more trips. I would climb more mountains, swim more rivers, watch more sunsets... I would eat more ice-cream and less beans. I would have more actual troubles and fewer imaginary ones. You see, I am one of those people who lives prophylactically and sanely and sensibly, hour after hour, day after day. Oh, I have had my moments and, if I had to do it all over again, I'd have more of them. In fact I'd try to have nothing else. Just moments, one after another, instead of living so many years ahead each day. I have been one of those people who never goes anywhere without a thermometer, a hot water bottle, a gargle, a raincoat, and a parachute. If I had it to do over again, I would go places and do things and travel lighter than I have.

If I had my life to live over, I would start bare-footed earlier in the spring and stay that way later in the fall. I would play hooky more. I wouldn't make such good grades except by accident. I would ride on more merry-go-rounds. I'd pick more daisies. ❜

Nadine Stair

Summary and action

The message in this chapter is: be kind to yourself and use your common sense to keep you fit and well emotionally, mentally and physically.

Further optional reading

Jacqueline Atkinson – *Coping with stress at work* – published by Thorsons
Leslie Kenton – *Passage to Power* – published by Vermillion

Action

What action are you now going to take to ensure your stress levels stay healthy?

Here are some suggestions:
- pick up again, or do with new enthusiasm, any stress-relieving techniques you have used successfully in the past
- use the two-minute exercises to overcome nerves, relax or concentrate
- ask friends about what works for them
- take some 'me' time

Write yours here:

Specific Action   **By When?**

Profile *Anita McGeough*

Job Title: Member
Organisation: Newry and Mourne Women's Group

I'm 41 and live in Hilltown, a small town in the
Mourne Mountains in Northern Ireland. I have three
adult children aged 23, 22, 19 and I've been a single parent for 18 years.
I'm a Protestant but I brought my children up as Catholics because I married
a Catholic man.

I'm happier now than I've ever been in my life. I feel very settled and content
and this is because over the past four years I've been working on my
personal development. Part of this is as a result of doing the Springboard
Programme. The trainer was a very positive role model and I could see that
being confident was achievable. The support and encouragement from other
participants was also very important to me. I could see how they were
developing as well — we were so alike in so many ways! It was encouraging
to see that whilst the detail of our lives may have been different, the big
picture was the same.

It hasn't always been this way for me. Life was difficult as a child — my father
suffered from depression and my mother wasn't supportive either of him or
towards her three daughters. My sisters and I were always helping each other
— we didn't realise it at the time but we were actually carrying each other
through a very challenging period in our lives.

My father committed suicide when I was 16 and for years, without realising it,
this event cast a shadow over me.

Within a year of my father dying I fell pregnant with my first child. I'd been
seeing a Catholic and until I was almost five months pregnant I couldn't tell
my mother. My sister always stood by me and she got me through the
sarcasm and rudeness about my situation and my future husband. I got
married — and life got worse.

I suffered physical, mental and emotional abuse at the hands of an adulterous alcoholic. I had to be strong for my children because they had to be looked after – my children come first. My sisters were supportive and they knew what was going on because I'd told them. As often as possible one of them would be with me – that way I knew my husband wouldn't be as bad – but eventually he was openly abusive and violent.

I left him on the advice of a Catholic Priest who told me that I had to get away. I'd always lived in hope – I thought my children needed a father – but I knew in my heart they didn't need a father like this. The children were five, four and one. Even after my husband left and we were separated he caused a lot of trouble. For a while we were prisoners in our home.

Soon I needed to work to earn some money. I was under a lot of stress working and managing a growing family. I didn't have a car and buses are infrequent in rural Ireland so time was short.

After four years something had to give – and I suffered severe depression. I was the lowest that I have ever been in my life. I took medication but interestingly around this time I began to realise the power of nature in helping me to cope. I took long forest walks, went beach combing and listened to the sea. It made me feel free of worries and deeply relaxed.

After a while, I tried doing some part-time work which I really enjoyed. I did a personal development course and began to realise everything I had going for me. I read books on subjects I was interested in and met other women – who all had a story to tell.

Things are different now. I look after myself in every way and I take time for me. I now believe in God after having lost all faith. I'm no longer doing things just to keep others happy and my friends tell me they see a big change for the better. I know now that I'm a nicer person than I used to be. I've learned a lot about myself, worked on my positives and I continue to 'dump' the bits of me which I don't like.

I'm taking time out from planning ahead. I've always wanted to work with animals but I'm quite content with how things are at present and will plan and set goals when I'm ready.

Learnings

- value the simple things in life
- other women are enormously supportive
- do what makes you happy
- live your life for you

10

Managing Your Image and Visibility

Objectives
- to promote a positive image of you
- to achieve the visibility you need to match your values and achieve your goals

This chapter is important because

- good performance is not enough
- people need to know what you're doing
- impressions count
- your good performance needs to be seen

Contents
- good image lets people see your good performance
- the image spectrum
- your customers and stakeholders
- your image
- your message
- your public relations campaign
- your exposure/visibility
- be positive
- be memorable!
- summary and action
- profile of Rachael Gilbert

Good image lets people see your good performance

Most of us feel better about ourselves when our good performance is being recognised, but recognition only comes when people can see how well you are doing.

So even if your goal is clear to you, your image may prevent others seeing you in ways that match your goals.

By consistently staying late and conscientiously doing extra work Mia thought that she was creating an image which would help her promotion prospects. She believed she was demonstrating that she was committed, keen, and hard working. Unfortunately her director interpreted her behaviour as demonstrating that she was overstretched, unable to cope and obviously not ready for promotion.

The idea of building an 'image' may seem to suggest that you become a phoney, a superficial and manipulative person.

This is not true. The image to build is the true one. This means being more yourself and putting the best 'you' forward. People need to have the clearest picture of you so they know who you are, what you want and what you have to offer, so you're going to have to take the initiative, and tell them about you. They won't ask!

If you've been ignoring this aspect, it might explain why:
• you seem to do good interviews but never get the job
• your friends don't take your idea of setting up your own business seriously
• your ideas always get ignored
• you get taken for granted
• you've become a Flossie

The Image Spectrum

Your image is one of those things that is always with you – like your shadow it never goes away, is there for others to see and is a part of you. Even if you choose to do nothing about it, you will still have an image because everyone else will still have an impression of what sort of person you are.

The good news is that you can change and adapt your image, so that it supports and reinforces what you're trying to do, rather than contradicts or undermines your efforts.

Image is not just the clothes you wear, it's the whole impression you create every day in all aspects of your life. Find the image that has the right balance for you.

In finding the balance, consider the two extremes open to you:

- at one end of the scale is the person who does not consider her image at all and takes the view that her work alone will gain her the recognition and perhaps the promotion she'd like
- at the opposite end of the scale is the superficial person who is all image and has no solid skills, qualities and experience to back it up: a sham

So concerned with image that you lose your real self

Image to fit your values and goals

No concessions to image at all

To find where you feel comfortable in between these two extremes, you will be influenced by your values and your integrity, so it may help to look again at page 61 to clarify your values. It is important that you feel good about the image you project, and that it fits you, your goals and your values.

> *In essence, be yourself, but be sure to project an image that does you justice and fits with your ambitions.*

Janet Cameron

The rest of this chapter gives you opportunities to check your image against your goals and values using an approach which promotes you in ways that you approve of. The approach brings you the visibility you need to get your good performance recognised. It applies to work and to personal matters.

Before you start promoting your positive image, you need to gather raw material about yourself and how others see you. A great deal of the work that you've done in the workbook so far contributes to this. You may find it useful to ask for further feedback on the impression you create both at home and at work.

Your customers and stakeholders

Customers are people who use your services. For example: managers, colleagues, family, potential employers and partners.

Stakeholders are people whose lives are affected by the things you do and the goals you set. For example: partners, bosses, friends, children.

Each has different needs. Try putting yourself in their shoes, and really understanding what their situation is:
* what are their needs?
* what do they really care about?
* what's in it for them, if they help you?

Photocopy the next page before you write on it and then build up your notes about what your customers and stakeholders really need. Then you can decide whether or not you are in the market to supply it!

Work through at least two examples of people whose needs you are considering meeting – the customers and stakeholders.

Fill out the next page or keep separate notes in a safe place.

Needs File

Name: *Lorna McIntosh*

Position: *Marketing Manager*

Needs: *People with lots of bright ideas who can manage others. Lots of prestige. Needs to be supported in doing things differently. Needs to be promoted soon – she's got stuck.*

Especially values: *People who make her laugh. People who get on with things by themselves. Experience in Sales.*

Likely attitude: *So-so. She either likes you or not. Patchy record on appointing non-graduates.*

Needs File

Name:

Position:

Needs:

Especially values:

Likely attitude:

Needs File

Name:

Position:

Needs:

Especially values:

Likely attitude:

Needs File

Name:

Position:

Needs:

Especially values:

Likely attitude:

Your image

Remember the research by Professor Albert Mehrabian which shows that the ways people receive messages from you fall into three categories?

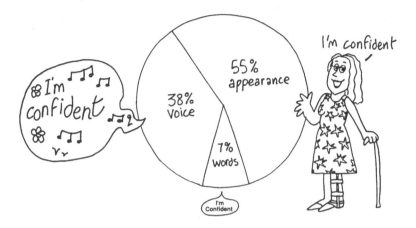

These statistics apply particularly where the whole message from you is not in tune or consistent. The words, the voice and the appearance have to match.

More than half the impression you create is in how you look. This is something we are all very aware of when we are consciously trying to create an impression – most of us wear special clothes to interviews, and dress up for special occasions.

However, people are piecing together their impression of you all the time so, if you want your message to be strengthened, it needs to be consistent.

Imagine walking into a roomful of people who you don't know. You immediately gain an impression of who the central characters are, who are in the supporting roles, and how everyone is feeling. The visual clues are:
- their posture
- whether people look you in the eye
- how expensive/old/new/tidy/untidy their clothes look
- their liveliness
- whether they smile
- the expression on their face

- hairstyle
- how colourful their hair/clothes/make-up are
- accessories, such as earrings, glasses, briefcase, etc.
- their mannerisms

It's not enough to have the right clothes, you also have to wear them with style and confidence! But what are the right clothes? Think about your key customers. Do you know what they're looking for?

Clothes codes vary from organisation to organisation and change over time. A very useful rule-of-thumb is 'dress for the role you're aiming to achieve'.

If you wear a uniform then you may have little or no choice, in which case all the other aspects of your image become more important. You can at least make sure that your uniform is clean and smart and that you choose the available options that suit you best.

Morag is a 27-year-old bright, ambitious graduate secretary. She talked about moving onward, sideways, anywhere, but she always got the same response – an indulgent smile and a shut door. In frustration, she sought feedback and discovered that people thought she was about 20 and not ambitious. She also discovered that her long, loose hair, frumpy clothes, and fresh, round face were all contributions to her little girl image.

She resolved to smarten up, had her hair re-styled and experimented with clothes. A new briefcase replaced her elderly bag, and Morag found that people took her aspirations more seriously and that her new image matched what she thought about herself.

 Dress as if you mean business. Coco Chanel once said that if a woman is poorly dressed you notice the clothes, if she's well dressed you notice the woman. ,

Vikki Worthington

JUDGE FOR YOURSELF

Rate how much your image is contributing to achieving your goals by scoring as follows:

1 – urgently needs attention – definitely holding me back
2 – making it difficult
3 – some improvement would help
4 – neither positive or negative
5 – helping rather than hindering – but could be improved
6 – positive impact
7 – perfect

	1 – 7		1 – 7
clothes:		weight	
tidiness		height	
style		posture	
quality		cleanliness	
age		smile	
shoes:		facial expression	
tidiness		sparkle in the eyes	
style		zest and energy	
quality		positive words	
age			
hair:			
style		workspace:	
colour		tidiness	
		style	
glasses, style			
accessories		emails	
handbag		diary/filofax	
jewellery		briefcase	
nails			
make-up			

Is this the impression that you want to create?

Decide which of these factors are important to you – add others that are appropriate for your:

- values
- goals
- current situation
- aspirations
- visibility – focus on how you are at:
    - telling people what you do well
    - putting yourself across positively at interviews
    - presentations
    - negotiations
    - phoning people to keep in touch

Label the spokes of the wheel with your important criteria as shown in the example. Mark your level of satisfaction with each item on the scale. Join up all the marks. See where you need to take action to bring imbalances up to strength.

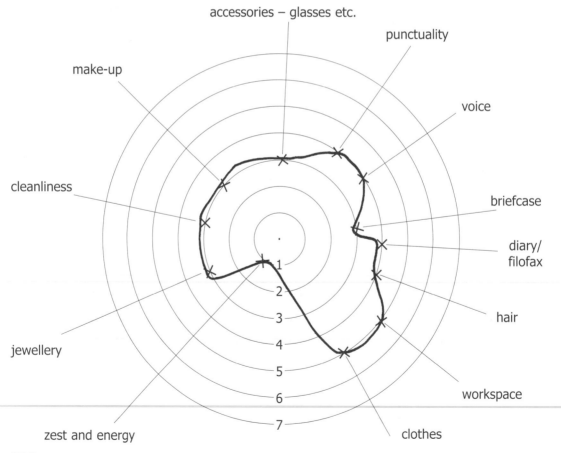

THE IMAGE WHEEL

1 – urgently needs attention – definitely holding me back

2 – making it difficult

3 – some improvement would help

4 – neither positive or negative

5 – helping rather than hindering – but could be improved

6 – positive impact

7 – perfect – is in line with values/beliefs

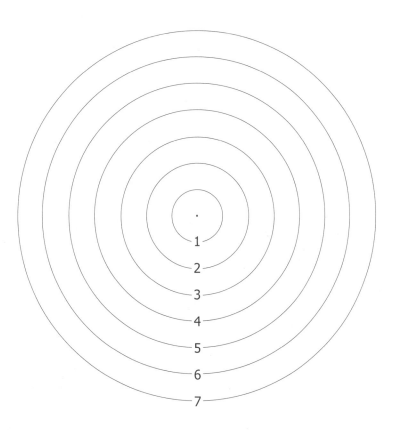

MEDITATION

Sit quietly and think about each colour of the rainbow:

> *violet*
>
> *indigo*
>
> *blue*
>
> *green*
>
> *yellow*
>
> *orange*
>
> *red*

Picture in your mind's eye for each, your preferred shade of each colour – a flower or something else from nature in that colour, then imagine yourself wearing that colour, would it be just a tiny bit of colour or a larger amount? See what comes to mind.

Your message

If you were selling a product you would decide on the message that needs to be put across and then choose the right medium. Chapter 11 looks into your opportunities to put yourself across in application forms, CVs and the like. The message you put across should:

- address the needs of your customers and stakeholders
- demonstrate the benefits
- prove results with evidence
- be positive
- be memorable

Your public relations campaign

Free gifts and demonstrations are ways of letting the customer try out the product without paying for it, in the hope that he/she will then want to buy it.

Some organisations offer secondments, job shadowing or attachments between departments – this is an opportunity for you to demonstrate to a possible new customer how great you are, as it lets them try you out, and also lets you try them out, day-to-day.

Other ways of demonstrating how great you are, without anyone paying any extra money for you, are:
- volunteering to do things
- getting yourself onto project groups
- organising social events
- having bright ideas

There is a fine line between this positive PR and being walked all over. Remember that you're doing this to demonstrate your skills and abilities. The moment you feel you're being taken for granted is the moment to review your strategy.

Keep the public relations going by making sure you tell people about the 'new improved you' when you have new skills, qualifications, additional experience or a greater commitment to what you're doing. Widen the scope of your public relations campaign to match your new goals.

Your exposure/visibility

Harvey Coleman's statistics (see page 41) show that 60% of whether you get promotion or recognition depends on your visibility, so it's worth thinking about.

Visibility means people knowing your
- name and face
- personality
- achievements
- potential

Some ways of doing this are:
- extending your contacts
- keeping up existing contacts
- getting involved in social/sports activities

- organising things
- writing articles for newsletters
- getting yourself in the internal newspaper/news-sheet
- speaking up on courses/at meetings
- being memorable – for whatever reason

How are people going to remember you? You'll have to tell them that you exist, that you're good, and what you want. And you'll probably have to tell them over and over again. It's a matter of grabbing every opportunity to remind people about you and your work.

Demonstrate the benefits

Very often, people describe themselves solely in terms of what they are. Talking in terms of benefits means adding how these aspects of yourself will benefit the customer and stakeholder.

Write down at least four features of yourself and work out the corresponding benefit:

Feature about me
(quality, experience, circumstances, etc)

Benefit to the customer
(what it does positively for her/him)

Most people do not promote themselves in this way. They support their application for a job, their proposal for a revised holiday rota or whatever, by emphasising how it would help them, without considering the effect and potential benefits to those they're trying to influence.

From now on, stop and put yourself in the other person's shoes.

Prove the results with evidence

When products are advertised, the manufacturers always focus on the results you will get from using a particular brand – it washes cleaner, is kinder to hands, and so on! Promote yourself in the same way with the messages you give about you. The more specific and clear you are with the evidence about what you do, the more effective your message will be.

Work out at least four examples of real evidence of how good you are:

Feature about me   **Prove it with evidence**

Be positive

Adverts do not point out the things that are unhelpful about a product, or remind us of how the product doesn't work, but people do. It is not unusual to hear people say negative things like: 'This job is boring', rather than 'I'm ready for more responsibility'.

Develop five really good, positive things to say about yourself and be able to back them up with evidence:

1.

2.

3.

4.

5.

Be memorable!

Things about you that make you different or special in some way also make you more memorable. These things are useful ingredients in your positive message and will make you:

- stand out
- preferable to the competition
- be very convincing
- better
- new and fresh
- special
- different
- unique
- best
- and above all memorable

Think of one thing about you that makes you memorable:

Alison was recently asked to give a short talk to another department. Afterwards the organiser sent her an email congratulating her on her good presentation skills.

Alison also forwarded the email to her immediate boss and her boss's boss. It then went up the line. A few days later she had six congratulatory emails in her inbox and Alison had successfully increased her exposure at a more senior level.

Meetings are another opportunity to make yourself and your views known. However, meetings can be fraught with difficulties and it is all too easy to be overlooked and become invisible.

If this tends to happen to you, remember 'The Mouse at the Meeting' law. This says that unless you say something within the first 10 minutes of the meeting, the chances are that you won't say anything at all. Watch the Mouse at the Meeting law at work – there's a lot of truth in it!

Make a point of speaking up within those all-important 10 minutes – anything to get yourself heard and noticed and to break the ice. You'll then find it much easier to speak up later on.

Some ideas that have worked for other women are:
• checking out the agenda or the objective of an item on it
• building on someone else's point
• agreeing with or checking understanding on someone else's point

PUT YOURSELF ACROSS POSITIVELY

Give a two-minute positive talk about yourself.

If you're not used to speaking positively about yourself, try practising with a group of family, friends or colleagues, or if that's not possible, record it and play it back the following day. If others join in, give each other feedback on how positively you come across and where you let yourself down.

This is an opportunity to really blow your own trumpet, so be as outrageous as you like! Get feedback on:
• what you felt was positive about the way you came across
• what you felt was negative about the way you came across
• where you felt you sold yourself short
• were you being modest?
• were you believable?
• were you over the top?
• what did you learn from or have reinforced by this exercise?

So what?

Having looked at aspects of your image, what do you want to do about it? Nobody goes around thinking of all these things all the time, but it is important to be clear and consistent in your message, or you run the risk of confusing your customers and stakeholders.

This takes time and effort. Every campaign needs investment and commitment at the beginning to get it moving. You may now be facing spending money on new clothes or a new haircut, or going to an exercise class.

Take small steps, and persevere. People may joke the first day you turn up with a new hairstyle, or express yourself positively. Doing things differently may make you vulnerable to jibes and sarcasm, but stick to it. People's memories are very short, and your new way of talking about yourself won't be considered worthy of a joke in a couple of weeks.

Summary and action

In this chapter you've looked at why image building is important and you've thought about your own image. The image to project is the real you, so that people can really see you and what you can do. The next chapter gives you practical tips about presenting yourself well and appropriately.

YOUR PERSONAL RESOURCE BANK

Go to page 275 and add your benefits and evidence.
On page 276, add the things that make you special and/or different.

Further optional reading

Eleri Sampson – *The Image Factor* – published by Kogan Page
Diana Mather – *Imageworks for Women* – published by Thorsons

Action

What action are you now going to take to develop your image?

Here are some suggestions:
- throw out things that don't fit your new image
- make a point of speaking up more at the next meeting that you attend
- let people know about your aspirations
- dress for your goals
- make contacts in a different part of the organisation

Write yours here:

Specific Action   **By When?**

Profile *Rachael Gilbert*

Job Title: Regional Manager
Organisation: Commission for Social Care Inspection

I was bullied through most of my school days. Not in a physical way but by words and social isolation. I was tall for my age, overweight, had huge boobs and frizzy hair. To avoid school I'd be sick or get off the school bus before it arrived at school. When I was at school I was a troublemaker and joined a gang of girls who were also different in the way they looked and behaved. Together we pushed school boundaries, were disruptive and at times abusive to both teachers and other children. By the time I left school, after a number of suspensions, I had one qualification (in history) to my name.

With this lack of qualifications further learning was out of the question so I needed to find a job, 'sign on' – or continue to hang about with my girlfriends. By this time most of my girlfriends had been expelled from school and were heavily involved in drugs and alcohol. One friend was working as a prostitute in Ipswich. Their lifestyle seemed easy – hanging about in the local launderette eating chips from the local chippy and not worrying about anything. My parents were good people and always had Christian values and standards. Maybe this influenced me or maybe I suddenly realised that if I wanted more out of life I needed to leave my friends, get off my backside and take responsibility for my future. I found an administrative job in the Prison Service and worked hard. I met new friends and through them learned how to go about studying and gaining useful qualifications.

The Prison Service was a good employer – it offered many learning opportunities and I spoke with my manager as well as my colleagues to find out what was on offer and what would meet my needs. However, it was a tough environment – male dominated and I still had a low opinion of my body and myself. I had to fight this all day, every day. I had one relationship whilst working at the prison, it lasted four years. Despite my bravado, my boyfriend realised I was an insecure person and had issues with my body. Although not deliberately cruel, he was unable to support me and often made me feel worse about myself. When the relationship ended, I thought my life would too and my confidence was at an all time low. Although we had bought the house together, when we split up my boyfriend remained living in our home and couldn't/wouldn't move so I had to leave. The house was sold quite soon afterwards – he had what profit there was and I returned home to my parents. Fortunately, I still had my job. I focused upon building a career and undertook a postgraduate diploma in Human Resource Management. I graduated after two years of study and my family were very proud of me.

After 13 years with the Prison Service I knew the day had come to leave my safety and work somewhere else. This was a very tough decision to make. I loved the people and the work but the job was no longer challenging and I needed to learn and grow. It was a huge step for me because the job and the people made such a difference to my confidence and had given me opportunities to learn about myself and what I was capable of – I felt encouraged and supported to try new things, be creative and innovative. However, I realised I liked to learn new things and be challenged. I was curious about just how far I could go and what exciting people and opportunities were waiting.

I currently work as a regional manager for the Commission for Social Care Inspection in Cambridge. I am very happy and have to pinch myself to check it's real! There have been a number of times in my life when I've made choices. Instead of just sitting around waiting for something exciting to happen I've taken charge. Life really is what you make it. I still have issues about my body but I've learnt to live with them and appreciate the other special gifts I have to offer. At a conference recently the facilitator talked about life decisions. He said that our life is a story and every minute we write a sentence, every day we write a page. I'd like my life to be an exciting story, where each chapter tells of happiness, success and achievements. Sure, I expect there to be days that are grey, but I know I can end the chapter there and start a new one. What will your story be?

Learnings

- have faith in yourself
- take yourself out of your comfort zone
- value ALL you have to offer
- life is what you make it

> *She who gets hired is not necessarily the one who can do the job best, but the one who knows the most about how to get hired.*

Natasha Josefowitz – *Paths to Power*

Presenting the Best You

Objective   • to put your own message across effectively

This chapter is important because

- your image and exposure contribute to your getting the job
- the application gets you the interview
- casual conversations can give lasting impressions
- your image is being built every day
- many organisations have an open system of competition

Contents
- applying for jobs
- curriculum vitae
- covering emails/letters
- interviews
- other formal conversations
- summary and action
- profile of Lorna Jackson

If you want to move yourself on to the next step, the messages you generate need to have a positive effect. A good application gets you the interview, a good interview gets you the job; the way you put yourself across day-to-day builds your own public relations campaign.

This chapter is a practical one, full of tips and do's and don'ts. They are all straightforward common sense, but as so often with common sense, it's good to be reminded. It covers the key elements of job applications.

Applying for jobs

Whether you're applying for something internally or from outside, at some point you'll encounter a written application process, be asked for your CV and experience an interview. Don't be put off by unclear job descriptions or vague adverts – use all the work you've just done in Chapter 10 as your raw material and think of a job application as the means for communicating it.

The Hay Group's 'Women's Work' report in 2006 reveals a significant gap in motivation and ambition levels between men and women, as well as fundamental differences in what drives the sexes in the workplace.

According to the study, men are 73% more likely than women to describe to themselves as highly motivated at work. More than half of men (54%) describe themselves as ambitious, compared to just 42% of women.

Men are also 62% more likely to be doing their dream job than women, with two thirds (59%) of men stating their job is well matched to their skills and abilities, compared to just two fifths (41%) of women.

Women believe that they would be as much as 46% more productive if they were doing a job they loved, and up to a third more productive with better training. *Source: www.haygroup.co.uk*

HR professionals indicate that women don't apply for jobs because they don't feel they fit all the criteria perfectly. The same people also tell of how men tend to adopt the opposite attitude – if you've got one of the requirements mentioned, it's worth a try. So is it that women aren't ambitious, lack confidence or have an unrealistic view of how they need to be to be ready for the next job? Have a go anyway and you may surprise yourself by getting the job and then finding that you are good at it!

Source: www.haygroup.co.uk

Applying from outside

If you're applying from outside the organisation do your homework e.g.

- check out the organisation's website to get information and some clues about the tone or style your application needs e.g. their image, tone, products, services, what they say about working for them, annual results, etc.
- visit the Head Office or a branch and pick up any literature you can e.g. annual report, newsletter, etc.
- read the relevant trade/industry magazines or websites and familiarise yourself with current topical issues
- talk to anyone you know who knows someone who works there, or in a similar organisation
- get an application form as early as possible, so you can be thinking about the format and learning more about how the organisation works
- experience the organisation in whatever way that you can, e.g. walk through the premises if they are open to the public or buy something as a customer

Written applications

Tailor each one specifically to the job you are applying for.

Some nuts and bolts

- get it checked for spelling and sense
- avoid gimmicks and unusual fonts
- be consistent in the way you present information, i.e. starting with the present and moving into the past
- make a copy for your interview preparation
- make sure you have followed any specific instructions, e.g. provide 3 copies of your full application

Getting your message across

- specific selection of the job description or advert
- make it results orientated, not just a recitation of what you are/were responsible for
- only put information that supports your case
- anticipate what they're looking for and address this head on
- be ENTHUSIASTIC
- use every space to tell them what you want to tell them
- make yourself different, e.g. instead of 'cooking' as an interest, be more specific - 'Thai cookery'. Instead of 'reading' – 'the novels of Kate Grenville'
- aim to influence the content of your interview by what you put on your application form
- if you know the organisation works with competencies then give evidence to prove your ability in the required competency areas
- make it clear that you have read the job description thoroughly and if you have been to talk to someone already doing the job, or to other people in the organisation, refer to your conversations
- don't be afraid to leave out personal details, e.g. marital status.
- translate your organisational or professional jargon so that the reader can relate to what you're saying
- because of age discrimination legislation there is no need to give your age – add it only if it helps your application

GET YOUR RESULTS ACROSS

Practise describing your last two jobs in terms of results. Do not be modest.

Job Title   **Results**

Curriculum vitae

Organisations often ask you to apply by sending your curriculum vitae. This is your opportunity to write your own sales material. Your CV is, literally, the story of your life, so it's up to you what you say and how you tell the story.

There is also no such thing as a standard CV – you will probably need to rewrite it and pitch it differently for every application. In addition, you may have a basic CV for networking which you feel represents you generally. Check out your CV against the tips that follow.

Nuts and bolts

Follow the guidelines already given, plus:
- keep it concise, four pages or less if possible
- make sure it's well laid out and easy to read

- show your first draft to someone who will give you constructive feedback
- be prepared to rewrite it several times

Content

- start with your name, address, work and home telephone numbers and email
- education with dates and qualification, with the best bits first. This can go after your career history if it's not your strong point
- employment – start with your most recent work, as it's likely to be the one of most interest to the reader, and then work backwards
- describe career breaks as you would a period of paid employment. Refer to them as, for example; 'managing a home' and describe what you did; 'organised finances, managed changing priorities,' etc.
- think 'portfolio' career if you have a mixture of experiences. This may be something that you consciously work on extending, or a pattern that you identify with the benefit of hindsight
- give each job title and department or company. Outline your responsibilities in one sentence for the most recent jobs. Follow this with a list of three to six notable achievements to prove how good you were. Jobs more than 15 years ago simply need the job title, organisation and dates
- include other information only if it helps your case, e.g. achievements outside paid employment
- conclude with items to list under 'interests'. Select them carefully, and make them interesting and different

If you have an old CV, compare it with someone else's and consider what you could have done better.

YOUR PERSONAL RESOURCE BANK

Turn to page 277 now and enter the key details you'll need to write any CV. It will help to prevent missing the deadline for an application while you find the key data.

Covering emails/letters

CV's and application forms do not, strictly speaking, need covering emails/letters, as they more or less speak for themselves. However, we suggest you use every opportunity to promote yourself and make yourself different, so always send a short personalised email/letter:

- maximum of one side of A4
- refer them to the best bits of your CV or application form
- condense your sales pitch into one short paragraph and tell them what's best or special about you
- EXPRESS ENTHUSIASM – it's a rare ingredient!

Interviews

All your work in this book will be excellent preparation for job interviews. Revise any chapters you consider will be important in applying for a particular job, check your personal resource bank and in particular take any action you need to on your image:

- refer back to the job description or advertisement. Use your skills audit on page 80 to see how you fit
- don't be put off if you don't fit all the criteria. Job adverts are written for the perfect person, who rarely exists. When it gets to the interview, they're looking for the best person from the ones who've applied
- consider the interviewers' needs – what are they looking for? Revise your exercise on the customer on pages 217-218
- what will have been sparked off in their minds by reading your application? For example if you've put down some very impressive achievements, they may want to know how you went about them, or what you enjoyed most about them
- how could what you say be misinterpreted? For example, if you overdo your enthusiasm to learn new things, it could be interpreted that you may not pay attention to the run-of-the-mill aspects of the job
- an interview is a two-way process – ask questions you could not have found answers to by your own research. Do not ask questions about things you should have discovered for yourself. Take a notebook into the interview and don't be afraid to refer to it or take notes on what you are told

- be prepared to let them know what you're good at – that's what interviews are about
- appear calm – the interviewer(s) may also be observing how you deal with the stress of an interview

About the practical arrangements

- if possible, discover where you come in the order of the day. If you are the 10th person they've interviewed that day, you'll need to pep up your performance to make yourself memorable. Equally so if you're the first – they'll still be settling down, and will 'warm up' on you
- find out how long you've got, so you can keep an eye on the time and ensure that you've said all your main points before time runs out
- plan your journey – aim to catch the earlier train or bus to get you there on time in case there are delays, and allow traffic or puncture time if you're driving

About you

- think about your appearance – refer back to Chapter 10. You need to look comfortable in yourself and as though you fit the job/role you're applying for. Wear something that you feel good in and associate with success
- deal with nerves – the butterflies don't go away, but you can get them to fly in formation! Nerves help give you an edge – and sharpen you up. Go back to Chapter 9 to find hints and tips on getting your nerves under control
- get to know your nerves and the effect they have on you. You can then develop strategies to accommodate them, such as:
  - if your mind goes blank, have the main points you want to make noted down
  - if you get nervous, get there early enough to discover where the 'Ladies' is, and give yourself a chance to get more comfortable
  - if you get a blotchy neck, wear a high-necked shirt or sweater
  - do the breathing exercise on page 200

What you'll be asked

There's no set formula or list of guaranteed questions. Think about questions you may be asked specifically about your ability to do the job, the selection criteria in the job description, questions that are topical, and questions that expand on the messages you've put on your application form or CV.

Don't take the questions at face value – think about what's behind the question.

Take your time before answering. Have a moment of silence rather than waffling until you've realised what you want to say!

For some posts be ready to complete a psychometric assessment before the interview – possibly on the same day. These are used increasingly and are there to reveal your strengths and good qualities for the job, and are not there to catch you out or snoop on you. Grab the opportunity, complete the test openly and honestly and welcome the valuable feedback you'll get from it. If they don't automatically give you feedback – ask for it.

Practise

Practise with a friend, colleague or another woman working through this book. It helps your nerves to say some of the 'blow your own trumpet' things out loud before the big day, so that you feel more comfortable with them.

Keep applying for jobs, to raise your visibility and build up your experience of interviews. Who knows, you may surprise yourself!

Compare notes with friends and colleagues to discover which topical questions are being asked currently.

Remember

- you have power in these situations – you can influence how your message is received in the way you put it across
- you are not being assessed on your value as a human being, you are

being assessed for your suitability for a specific job, secondment, project or course

 They won't know how good you are unless YOU tell them!

MEDITATION

Before you go for an interview use any of the breathing and relaxation techniques that have been given so far. Take quiet and relaxing time to imagine yourself actually doing the job.

Picture the building or the site that you will work in, imagine what the routine of a day will be, think about the people that you are likely to meet in a day.

- What will they want from you?
- How will you meet their needs?
- Which of your values will you be fulfilling?
- What qualities, skills or experience will you need for the job?
- Where have you already used these qualities or skills?
- How did you gain the experience?

Allow your mind to give you as complete a picture as you can and when you finish visualising all these things write down anything you may find useful for the interview.

Afterwards

Whether you get the job or not, always ask for feedback on your application, interview performance and, if applicable, your psychometric assessment or any other tests you are given. Most interviewers are happy to do this over the phone and have been known to offer people alternative jobs. It may be that you did really well, but simply weren't the appropriate person for that particular job.

Asking for feedback:
- makes you memorable
- shows them that you take your aspirations seriously

- reminds them of your enthusiasm
- nearly always makes you feel better
- helps you know yourself better

Other formal conversations

Other formal conversations are when you talk to your manager or another key person, in a situation such as an appraisal interview, a target-setting session, a performance review, staff-assessment interview or career development interview. Alternatively, you may find yourself in more casual conversations over a cup of coffee by the drinks machine or in a corridor, where it's just as important to create a good impression.

Use all these situations to practise all the points about putting yourself across positively, and remember:
- you are building your image all the time
- all conversations contribute to the impression others have of you
- talk about your aspirations and achievements realistically not modestly
- ensure your message is positive

When someone asks how your work is use phrases such as 'I've outgrown my job' rather than 'I'm bored' or 'I'm looking for something new' rather than 'It's the same old stuff'.

Here are three questions people often ask, so make some notes here for your positive replies:

'How are you getting on?'

'What are you doing these days?'

245

'What do you want to do next?'

Performance review or personal development planning interviews are a classic. How will your manager remember your particular achievements of almost a year ago, unless you remind them? It isn't being big-headed, it's being positive and self-confident.

Interviews and conversations are two-way processes, so do your preparation and go in there armed with your list of positive things to raise, e.g.
- ask for feedback on your eligibility for another job
- ask for training and development
- ask for support for a secondment or work shadowing
- list your achievements

Make a note here of things you want to raise:

After all, you've got nothing to lose – so have a go!

Summary and action

By writing job applications and CV's in positive, results-orientated ways you'll increase your chances of success.

By making your general conversation about yourself positive and enthusiastic you'll enhance your image on a day-to-day basis.

YOUR PERSONAL RESOURCE BANK

Make a note on page 276 of your progress with interviews.

Further optional reading/contacts

John Lees – *How to get a job you love* – published by McGraw Hill

Action

What are you going to do now to make sure you blow your own trumpet?

Here are some suggestions:
- get feedback from a friend or colleague on your last or next job application
- look at jobs in the newspapers and consider how you could transfer your skills to do those jobs – if you wanted to
- discuss with your boss what you want to achieve in your present job
- put your CV on the Internet

Write yours here:

Specific Action   **By When?**

Profile *Lorna Jackson*

Job Title: Social Care Learning and Development Manager
Organisation: Northamptonshire County Council

I was born long enough ago to remember the Bay City Rollers and Jimmy Osmond. I was the fifth child in our family but brought up as the middle child of three as my older brother and sister were a great deal older than me and my other siblings.

I grew up wanting to be a nurse but my careers advisor thought otherwise and told me not to bother and consider working in a factory instead. I thought that this was rather peculiar as I was in an 'A' stream class at school and there was no reason I shouldn't get good grades. It didn't dawn on me at the time that the careers advisor could be racist.

Despite this, I did go to college and these years were all about freedom. College was wonderful – adults who treated you like a human being and who, in turn, wanted to teach and enjoyed teaching (well, most of them).

From college I progressed to university after a break of two years – I needed to work during these two years to help support my mum. At university I studied public administration but by some twist of fate the degree changed part way through and became a degree in social work with sociology.

In 1993 I graduated from an East London university and took a locum post in an East London Hospital where I was a full-time SCBU (Special Care Baby Unit) Liaison Officer specialising in drug use in uterine babies.

Since then I have survived 11 years post-qualifying experience in child protection and fieldwork practice. In 2003 I gained a Masters Degree in Advanced Interprofessional Social Practice and during that time gave birth to my fourth child whilst completing the dissertation. My first child was born in 1991 so you do the maths!

Since making the leap into first line management I successfully applied for a Unit Manager post for a countywide Hospital Social Work Assessment Team at a regional hospital providing paediatric and maternity social work services. This included developing SCBUs, multi-agency teams and working alongside voluntary organisations and developing two further assessment posts fully funded by external agencies for SCBU and A&E (Accident and Emergency) departments.

Now I think I've arrived at my ideal job role as Learning and Development Manager responsible for Social Care Learning and Development. I applied for and was successful in gaining a position as Learning and Development Officer managing seven full time Training Officers across both Children and Families and Adult services.

I have since been promoted into the role of Social Care Learning and Development Manager responsible for managing 25 posts. I am also the lead officer for the children and young people's partnership project group and have produced a draft workforce reform strategy which has been published on the sector skills website as an exemplar of good practice.

This might sound exhausting but I haven't stopped there. I gone on to have my fifth child and have undertaken a portfolio of evidence for my Advanced Award in Social Work. There's a myth that your brain capacity shrinks when you're pregnant. However, this doesn't work for me and I hope I have proved that life doesn't necessarily have to end just because you have children!

I would be kidding if I didn't acknowledge it's hard work at times. Especially as I insist on those 'good old' family values like all sitting around a table to share a meal, that the children are in bed at a respectable hour and that I do my own housework and ironing (the latter a pet hate of mine!) However, it's rewarding knowing that I can make a difference in my children's lives and a difference in the lives of the children, young people and adults through the workforce my team supports by providing good quality learning and development opportunities.

So, what next? For the first time, I'm not really sure. I still want to learn Spanish. I also want to fulfil a dream and see parts of the States. I'd also love to cut an album – you never know. I believe the keys to success are to 'control', to 'influence' and to 'accept'.

Learnings

- pursue your dreams whatever anyone says
- be extraordinary! Without feeling the need to be wonder women (well not all the time anyway!)

Making It Happen

Objective
- to give you the support and encouragement to keep going

This chapter is important because

- you're approaching the end of this workbook
- this is the beginning of the rest of your life
- you make things happen for yourself
- it's your life – to be lived how you want it

Contents
- dealing with failure or mistakes
- building on success
- your energy and enthusiasm
- networking
- Springboard summary
- you have a choice
- action
- profile of Naseem Aboobaker

What have you done so far?
- you've worked your way through over 240 pages
- you've done lots of exercises – on your own and with others
- you've been asked all sorts of questions
- you've jotted down your thoughts on every subject under the sun

What does it all add up to?
- a load of rubbish?
- a lot of common sense?
- confirmation of what you already knew?
- a real eye-opener?

Whatever you think of this book, and wherever you are in your life, one thing is guaranteed:

None of this will make anything happen in your life unless you really want it to.

If you stretch yourself, you run the risk of failing or making mistakes, so consider your attitude to failure, and what your strategy will be for dealing with it.

Dealing with failure or mistakes

Failure is where something has an unsuccessful or disappointing outcome. A mistake is something you didn't mean to happen. Both can feel negative and yet can be a vital part of your success. There is a world of difference between saying to yourself 'oh dear, I didn't mean that to happen and I am disappointed' and 'I've failed' or even worse 'I'm a failure'.

Mistakes are normal, and women who are regarded as successful have usually made loads, learned from them and then had the determination to carry on or know when to stop.

 Perseverence is failing 19 times and succeeding the 20th.

Julie Andrews

Failure at something is almost inevitable at some point in life. It helps one see the need to keep trying new ways forward. Failure in one respect can open new doors to other possibilities. This means that a 'portfolio' career is increasingly a boon for survival. If one job or part of your work load fails to succeed, you have others to fall back on. When one grant falls through, go for another, perhaps of a different type. When my research contract was not renewed at one point, I went on to other grants and positions, including company directorships that not only paid well, but added a new dimension to my life. I took on a host of other positions, many voluntary and without salary (except for paying for transport) and these helped improve my life skills, extend my networks and expand my knowledge-base. My work in pressing for more women in SET*, such as WiSETI and Athena, all sprung from such an event.

Learning point: Never take a failure in one part of your life to be too discouraging. Such experiences can open doors to new and better positions. A portfolio career, acquiring a number of different part-time positions, or posts that require, for example, monthly meetings only, especially for women with families, can be the solution for a successful, more flexible working life.

Nancy Lane   * science, engineering and technology

Failure and mistakes

- stretch you
- sensitise you
- show people you aren't afraid of taking risks
- can move you forward or move you back
- may increase your choices of what you do next
- challenge you and make you stronger
- teach you about timing
- give you practice
- can be painful

In positive people, failure can bring out greater determination which, combined with their positive attitude, creates a winning combination.

LEARNING FROM FAILURE AND MISTAKES

Think back to what you regard as failure or mistakes in your life and with the benefit of hindsight, consider what they taught you. Many people say that what appeared to be a setback at the time often turns out to be a positive turning point in their lives.

Occasion   **What you learnt**

How have you dealt with failure in the past?

What worked well?

What do you want to do differently in the future?

Charles Rennie Mackintosh said: "There is hope in honest error; none in the icy perfections of the mere stylist". If you aren't making mistakes, you aren't trying hard enough.

Vikki Worthington
Researcher, Central Independent Television plc

Another part of dealing with failure positively is to be ingenious in the way you overcome the blocks that you meet. First of all:

Check you're using what's available

- find a secondment to provide the experience or skills that you need
- find out about grants, trusts, and scholarships which would get you new experience and new contacts, and where others would support you
- be alert to new projects and initiatives which could get you moving again
- consider moving sideways to enable you to come back at a higher level. Use your transferable skills to do this
- extend your contacts and ask their advice
- arrange informally to shadow someone whose job you want to find out about – it need only be for a day
- find a third choice where you're in an A or B situation. Not just a compromise but a real choice to break through

Doreen qualified in accountancy in her late-30s, when on her career break. When she tried to return to work she failed to get a job in accountancy because, while she had the qualifications, she had no experience. She overcame this by becoming the treasurer of the local Oxfam group and organised a spectacularly successful sponsored run. In her next application, Doreen was able to show how she had handled thousands of pounds in the last year. She got the job!

Rafia was never considered for promotion because she'd become indispensable where she was. Once she realised this, she made a point of developing one of her team members to be just as capable as she was, and freed herself to be promoted.

Building on success

Success:
- boosts your confidence
- tells you you've got it right for you
- shows people what you can do
- gives you energy
- happens every day
- encourages you
- speeds you up
- needs to be recognised – by you and others
- can make you complacent
- can spur you on to do more – even when it will be more difficult

Everyone has their own personal definition of success. Refer to yours on page 125.

Celebrate your successes

Don't skip this part because generally you don't celebrate. In that case there's all the more reason to consider it.

Celebrating is a very good way to show that you value yourself.
Celebrating:
- is fun
- gives you energy
- shows and re-enforces self-esteem
- is a reward
- establishes a milestone in your progress

You've almost finished this book. You've managed to find time in amongst everything else in your life to do the exercises – Congratulations!

What are you going to do to celebrate your achievements?

Your energy and enthusiasm

Along with failure and mistakes, determination is the other hallmark of the successful person, so consider for a moment how you're going to make the most of your energy and enthusiasm to keep going.

FIND ACTIVITIES TO REVIVE YOU

The things that energise you will be very personal. Here are some ideas that other women have mentioned. Are yours here?

long walks	a long bath
exercise class	a massage
an evening of TV	chat with a friend
day in bed alone	some domestic chores
day in bed with company	a swim
sunshine	sports
playing with the kids	being alone

Now add yours:

Which activities are your favourites?

Do you have a balance of activities between those:
- you do on your own and those you do with others?
- that cost nothing, very little or a lot?
- that take a long time or five minutes?

When did you last do these activities?

 Do a reviving activity daily – do one now!

Networking

Throughout this workbook we've encouraged you to renew old contacts and make new ones. If you have been working through the book in a group then we hope that you've been giving each other ideas and support all the way through. If not then we hope that you've been consciously extending your network to a wider range of people. Women often network easily for others (children, friends) and may need to enhance their networking for themselves and their development.

To network well you'll:
- support each other and boost confidence
- share problems and information
- think in a networking way so if you can't help someone, you'll think of who you know who can
- make sure you don't pull the ladder up on those coming up behind

- be objective, straightforward and tactful in your feedback to each other
- celebrate each other's successes and support each other in your failures
- still compete for the same jobs
- laugh and sometimes cry together
- strengthen each other by mutual support

The value of networking is summed up in this verse 'Support Systems':

> *My right hand is being held*
> *by someone who knows more than I,*
> *and I am learning.*
> *My left hand is being held*
> *by someone who knows less than I,*
> *and I am teaching.*
> *Both my hands need thus to be held*
> *for me – to be.*

Natasha Josefowitz – *Is This Where I Was Going?*

MEDITATION

All the way through the book we have been suggesting meditations and visualisations for you to enhance the work that you have been doing in each chapter. Now it is up to you to decide either to work here with your favourite one or to make up your own.

Just remember to make the quiet space, concentrate on your breathing and then allow yourself to picture a scene and stay with it or select a word, phrase or verse that you think will help you now.

Setting up a network

If two or three women agree to meet up for lunch to give each other ideas and support – that's a network! (Equally, many women have formed groups to network more formally and publicly). Many networks are well established and huge, such as the Women's Institute, or more specific such as British Association of Women in Policing. According to the Demos Report 2004, 'Girlfriends in High Places', new 'girl' networks are challenging the power of the 'old boys' network'.

If you want to set up a more formal network, this checklist will get you started:

1. What are your objectives?

2. Who will be eligible to attend?

3. Talk to your organisation and Trade Union if it's a network for women in that organisation.

4. When are you going to meet?

5. Where are you going to meet?

6. What is the role of men: as members, allies, speakers, etc? Refer back to your objectives.

7. What publicity do you need?

8. Give it a descriptive or catchy name.

9. Start small and let it grow.

10. Who's going to organise it?

11. Respond flexibly to the needs of the group.

12. Network with other networks – see Chapter 14.

13. Start now!

What are you going to do to extend and maintain your networks?

Springboard summary

The chapters of this book give you a self-development process that you can use over and over again, either on an ongoing basis, or when you are wanting to review and make changes. Go back and do any of the exercises, or work through any of the chapters again whenever you want to.

Your Personal Resource Bank (Chapter 13) is there for you to refer to whenever you need to. Keep it up to date and it will provide you with a compact and rich source of data to help you to:
• make a decision
• reassess yourself
• write a job application/CV
• go for an interview
• boost your confidence
• keep on track

In this workbook you have:
• prepared yourself
• assessed the environment you're in
• assessed yourself
• assessed the support from other people
• set your goals

Since your goals were set, you have:
• gained the information you need
• gained assertiveness skills to help you
• looked at your image and the signals you send out about yourself
• developed healthy stress strategies
• dealt with failure and success
• built your networks

How are you getting on?

If you've been working through the workbook in great detail then you have done a lot of work and covered some challenging issues.

Maybe you've worked through some bits, and skipped over others to keep up with your group, if you were working with one, or simply because they were less important to you. Or was it because they were too challenging?

If you've been reading the book without doing the exercises then we encourage you to go back and work through them, because what looks simple or obvious as you read it can be more important, meaningful, thought provoking or challenging when you actually do the work on it.

REVIEW YOUR OWN PROGRESS HERE

Did you achieve the objectives you set yourself on page 13:
- in full?

- in part?

Where did you feel challenged?

How did you meet the challenge?

What went really well and why?

Where did your support come from?

How far have you achieved the goals you set in Chapter 6?

What have you learnt that you will take into the future?

In which ways do you feel differently about yourself and your situation?

You have a choice

As you know, there is nothing magic in this workbook. All the strategies and techniques are common sense, born out of the experiences of the thousands of women we've met on courses and in our travels.

Doing all the things we've suggested in this workbook is not enough. You have to WANT to do it, and to continue to want to do it, so:

 You have a choice, every day, and every day can be a fresh start.

Every day you can decide whether to make the effort, take the risk, and take another step in your own journey. Every day you can decide not to – you can lose your energy and let it go. If you falter, you can pick yourself up again, dust yourself off and have another go – it's up to you.

You have total freedom in your choice

No one is going to make it happen for you, you have to make it happen for yourself, and every day you can renew your commitment freely – or not.

What you do and how you do it is entirely up to you. We would simply say – DO IT! We believe it's important that you do, because that way you will become more fully yourself and be the best you can be.

Live the life that you choose for yourself – not the life that your parents (or whoever brought you up) mapped out for you, or that your partner assumes for you, or that you seem to have fallen into. Make the choice, and then put it into action, through small practical steps, or big dramatic leaps – whatever fits you best.

Whatever it is that you decide to do – we wish you your own definition of success in doing it!

Nelson Mandela made the following words famous as the first black president of South Africa. His quotation came from the book 'Return to Love' by Marianne Williamson.

Our deepest fear is not that we are inadequate
Our deepest fear is that we are powerful beyond measure
It is our light, not our darkness, that most frightens us.
We ask ourselves, 'Who am I to be brilliant, gorgeous, talented, fabulous?'
Actually, who are you not to be? You are a child of God.
Your playing small doesn't serve the world.
There is nothing enlightened about shrinking so that other people won't feel insecure around you.
We are all meant to shine, as children do.
We are born to make manifest the glory of God that is within us.
It is not in some of us; it is in everyone.
And as we make our own light shine, we unconsciously give others permission to do the same.
As we are liberated from our fear, our presence automatically liberates others.

Action

What are you going to do now, to continue taking positive steps in your life?

 A journey of 1,000 miles starts with a single step.
Keep taking the steps!

Profile *Naseem Aboobaker, MBE*

Job Title: Project Director
Organisation: Mushkil Aasaan (Crisis Eased) Community Care for Families

Having endured an arranged marriage in which I had no say at the age of 20 years, I arrived in the UK as a young mother of 21 years on a cold and dark December morning. Not having been able to have any say in being uprooted to an alien environment, I began to nurture negative feelings of resentment and grief for what life could have been in the warm heart of Africa – Malawi.

These feelings were further exacerbated by being stuck in a claustrophobic small house doing household chores and serving traditional meals subserviently to a whole clan. There was no privacy to build a relationship with my husband. My only consolation was my lovely content baby – but there was a problem there as well, he was diagnosed with a right hemiplegia. My only contact with the outside world was to take my son for physiotherapy two to three times a week.

The whole clan was in culture shock – unable to make ends meet or find any positions having only been used to running their businesses. Finding it demeaning to claim welfare benefits or to be working for other people, things did not get any better for my husband. Not being able assert his position in a family business and becoming totally dependent on them, our relationship began to go downhill.

After numerous miscarriages, two more children and a disheartening sense of apathy at family unity and deteriorating values, my innermost feelings of this cannot be 'it' in life began to surface in episodes of crisis, violence and desperation. All I knew within me was there must be more to life – but what and how?

The crunch came when my husband chose to fall prey to the influences of promiscuity to have another woman. To this day, everything had been tolerated but this was something completely unacceptable to my very existence and an affront to the hardships borne for his family.

The clear and adamant decision to make the break coming from an oppressed, submissive, tired and ill mother of three was a shock to all, creating an international uproar as my traditional marriage had been one between two clans rather than two individuals. What followed was not any easier – years of unsuccessful mediation by family members, stigmatising, depriving of basic sustenance money, and threats of homelessness. The children were emotionally traumatised and made wards of court, so I was unable to move 'back home' and start afresh.

Finding the courage to seek help was an equally disillusioning experience. Statutory services had no understanding of what I was going through – police intervention would leave my husband more encouraged to be violent. I sought legal advice but solicitors were more concerned with the bureaucracies of legal aid and reluctant to challenge asian family business dynamics for basic sustenance. Social workers did not feel that there was anything wrong in a man having another woman. Refuge workers blamed the culture and the religion – the solution would be to shed the values and assimilate into peer society. Psychiatrists did not understand the importance of cultural family values – what were these 'red herrings'? Male dominated Mosques were a place of worship and it was not their role to get involved in family matters.

I continued to live in the matrimonial home under the threat of homelessness for 10 years until my sons partly inherited the property after years of legal proceedings. From two hours of paid work as a co-ordinator for mother-tongue language classes increasing to a part-time admin post, financial survival was imperative without any maintenance payments – so much for the famous Child Support Agency!

Where does a woman turn to? True to the saying that 'there is a seed of good in every calamity', help came in the form of emotional support to me and my children from a volunteer in the wider community. She remains a truest friend to this day and opened the doors in coming to terms with destiny, helping others in crisis and sharing whatever good there was. Capitalising on the strengths of each other this evolved into a range of activities and support networks for us and our children, nurturing a sense of belonging and alleviating isolation. Going from strength to strength in advocating for unmet needs this gave birth to a highly successful charity which has won many awards including Investors in People. It has created employment for 100 people who would not have otherwise ventured into the employment world and touched upon the lives of many families to effect change and empowerment. All of this from the floor of my front room!

Life has not been a bed of roses – but I can certainly say I've lived an enriched life, have had the most rewarding experiences and met truly wonderful people. Hopefully I'll be able to face my Creator and say I strived to live Truthfully.

The most painful lesson I've learnt however is that there is nothing that compensates sons for the vacuum left by absent fathers. My three sons struggled in isolation in their lives and paid the price of being loyal to their mother in the male-dominated cultural setting of the business world. It has taken immense efforts in anchoring them in their journeys of life and reconciling them with their blood ties, but we all continue to strive daily with the faith:

'And unto everyone who is conscious of God, He always grants a way out of unhappiness, and provides for that person in a manner beyond all expectation.' (Quran 65:2-3)

Learnings

- stand up for yourself and what you believe in
- never give up!
- pass on what you learn to others in need

13

Your Personal Resource Bank

Objective
- to compile a reference book of useful information about yourself for future use

Your Personal Resource Bank

This chapter gives you headings under which you build up your bank of useful data about yourself. It means that you keep all the overall facts and ideas about yourself in one place, and gives you material to refer to whenever you want to review or change anything in your life. It will be particularly useful to you when you:
- apply for a job
- prepare for an interview
- face a difficult life situation
- are faced with change
- want to reset goals
- write your CV
- make decisions
- want to revive your determination

Each chapter has valuable information for your personal resource bank. Here are handy references to key pages. Also record anything else you find useful. Write it here or start your own computer file for reference.

CHANGE

My usual responses to change at home and at work – pages 10-11

MY QUALIFICATIONS

School qualifications
e.g. CSEs, GCSEs, GCEs A, AS and S levels, Scottish Leaving Certificates:

Other qualifications taken at school
e.g. Duke of Edinburgh Award, Queen's Guide, life-saving certificates, music certificates:

College, art school or university qualifications

e.g. secretarial qualifications, RSA typing awards, degrees, post-graduate degrees,
City and Guilds, college diplomas, BTEC, NVQs, technical qualifications:

Courses attended where no formal qualifications were given at the end

Professional qualifications

Also include courses that you're part way through:

Qualifications I need/want to get in the future

Anything else?

Values

The things I value most highly – page 61

Achievements

The things I have achieved – page 72
The things I want to achieve – page 73

⌐*The achievement I'm particularly proud of is:*

Strengths and Weaknesses

The qualities that are my strengths – page 76
The qualities I'm working on keeping in balance – page 77

Skills

Pages 80-82

Transferable Skills

My best skills are: An example of using them well is:

In addition, other people say I am also good at:

People

People who are actively helping me now – pages 102-106

People who I am going to ask to help me are:

Information I've found out about contacts – page 109-110

GOALS

ASSERTIVENESS

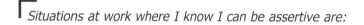 *Situations at work where I know I can be assertive are:*

Situations at home where I know I can be assertive are:

Situations where I know I can be assertive with myself are:

PRESENTING THE BEST YOU

Benefits and evidence from 'Managing Your Image' pages 226-227

Feature about me	Evidence of this	Benefit to others

Things that make me special or different are:

When I go for interviews, I know I'm good at:

The aspect I need to work on is:

MY WORK HISTORY

Dates	Organisation/ Department	Job Title	Achievements

MY WORK HISTORY

Dates	Organisation/ Department	Job Title	Achievements

MY WORK HISTORY

Dates	Organisation/ Department	Job Title	Achievements

MY WORK HISTORY

Dates	Organisation/ Department	Job Title	Achievements

OTHER THINGS I WANT TO KEEP A NOTE OF

14

Where Can I Find...?

Organisations

Organisations

The Authors
Campaigning Groups
Equal Opportunities and Human Rights
Health and Wellbeing
Lesbian Support
Study and Careers
Women's Networks
Working Mothers and Families

Books

Other books by the Authors of this book
Assertiveness
Disability Issues
Health
Personal Development
Relationships
Sexuality
Skills
Women's Issues

Some CDs

Useful Websites

Organisations

The Authors

Liz Willis and Jenny Daisley
The Springboard Consultancy
Tel: 01271 850828
Email: office@springboardconsultancy.com

www.springboardconsultancy.com

Campaigning Groups

Fawcett Society
Tel: 020 7253 2598
Email: info@fawcett.org.uk   **www.fawcett.org.uk**
Campaigning for changes in legislation to give women true equality. Also gives information. Founded during the suffrage movement in 1866.

National Alliance of Women's Organisations (NAWO)
Tel: 020 7490 4100
Email: nawo@nawo.org.uk   **www.nawo.org.uk**
Umbrella organisation for over 100 organisations and individuals based in England, concerned to ensure women gain access to their human rights, and to make equality between women and men a reality.

National Council of Women
Tel: 020 7354 2395
Email: ncwgb@danburystreet.freeserve.co.uk   **www.ncwgb.org**
Umbrella organisation – regional councils, information and lobbying.

RADAR
Tel: 020 7250 3222
Email: radar@radar.org.uk   **www.radar.org.uk**
Up-to-date information on disability issues.

Rights of Women
Tel: 020 7251 6577

Email: info@row.org.uk **www.rightsofwomen.org.uk**
Free legal advice and assistance for women.

The Suzy Lamplugh Trust
Tel: 020 7091 0014
Email: info@suzylamplugh.org **www.suzylamplugh.org**
The leading authority on personal safety: aiming to create a safer society and enable all people to live safer lives.

Womankind Worldwide
Tel: 020 7549 0360
Email: info@womankind.org.uk **www.womankind.org.uk**
Enabling women in developing countries to take greater control over their own lives by funding practical projects.

Working Families
Tel: 020 7253 7243
Email: office@workingfamilies.org.uk **www.workingfamilies.org.uk**
Job sharing and other flexible working arrangements. Information, publications, seminars and presentations.

Equal Opportunities and Human Rights

The Commission for Equality and Human Rights
Kingsgate House
66-74 Victoria Street
London SW1E 6SW **www.cehr.org.uk**
This Commission, set up in October 2007, is a Non-Departmental Public Body (NDPB) and independent influential champion whose purpose is to reduce inequality, eliminate discrimination, strengthen good relations between people and protect human rights. The CEHR takes an active role in helping to achieve change to benefit some of the most vulnerable and least well represented people in our society.
The CEHR brought together the work of three Commissions, the Commission for Racial Equality (CRE), Disability Rights Commission (DRC) and Equal Opportunities Commission (EOC).

The CEHR took on all of the powers of the existing Commissions as well as new powers to enforce legislation more effectively and promote equality for all. The Commission will champion the diverse communities that make up modern Britain in their struggle against discrimination.
It will also promote awareness and understanding of human rights and encourage good practice by public authorities in meeting their Human Rights Act obligations. New powers to take human rights cases will give a new arrow to the bow of many minorities who suffer discrimination.
The Commission covers England, Scotland and Wales. In Scotland and Wales statutory committees are responsible for the work of the CEHR.

TUC Equal Rights Department
Tel: 020 7636 4030
Email: info@tuc.org.uk **www.tuc.org.uk**
Provides useful publications on Equal Rights and deals with a wide range of equality issues.

The Wainwright Trust
Tel: 01920 821698
Email: wainwright.trust@btinternet.com

www.wainwright-trust@btinternet.com
Promotion of equal opportunities and elimination of discrimination on grounds of gender and race through grants for research, dissemination of good practice and the 'Breakthrough Award' for outstanding work in this field.

Women's National Commission
Tel: 0207 944 0585
Email: wnc@communities.gsi.gov.uk **www.thewnc.org.uk**
The official, independent, advisory body giving the views of women to the Government.

Health and Wellbeing

Al-Anon Family Groups
Tel: 020 7403 0888 (24-hour helpline)
Email: enquiries@al-anonuk.org.uk **www.al-anonuk.org.uk**

Al-Anon offers understanding and support for families and friends of problem drinkers, whether the alcoholic is still drinking or not. Alateen, a part of Al-Anon, is for young people 12-20 who have been affected by someone else's drinking, usually that of a parent. For details of meetings throughout the UK and Eire please contact the above.

Alcoholics Anonymous

Tel: 0845 769 7555 (national helpline)

Email: aanewcomer@runbox.com   **www.alcoholics-anonymous.org.uk**

Voluntary, international fellowship of people wishing to stop drinking. Provides anonymity, group support and a 12-step programme for recovery. See telephone directory for your local group.

All Women Count

Tel: 020 7482 2496

Email: allwomencount@crossroadswomen.net   **www.allwomencount.net**

International organisation campaigning for equality.

Breast Cancer Care

Tel: 020 7384 2984 Helpline: 0808 800 6000

Email: info@breastcancercare.org.uk   **www.breastcancercare.org.uk**

Information and support for women with breast cancer, their families, friends or partners.

Cruse Bereavement Care

Tel: 020 8939 9530 Day-by-day helpline: 0870 167 1677

Email: info@cruse.org.uk   **www.crusebereavementcare.org.uk**

Publications and national network and counselling for anyone bereaved. For free leaflet or mail order catalogue please send SAE to above address.

Disabled Living Foundation

Helpline: 0845 130 9177

Email: via website   **www.wlf.org.uk**

Offers impartial advice to public and professionals on equipment and assistive technology; also offers training and conferences for professionals.

Eating Disorders Association

Tel: 0870 770 3256

Email: info@b-eat.co.uk   **www.b-eat.co.uk**

Helps sufferers and their families. Literature, support groups and telephone counselling.

Elizabeth Garrett Anderson Hospital

Tel: 0845 155 5000   **www.nhs.uk** – select hospital by name

Self-referral clinic staffed by women for women. Provides a range of screening services.

i-Village   **www.ivillage.co.uk**

Online interactive network for women offering practical advice and support on wide variety of subjects.

Marie Stopes Clinic

Tel: 020 7574 7400

Email: info@mariestopes.org.uk   **www.mariestopes.org.uk**

Advice on all women's health issues.

National Association for Pre-menstrual Syndrome

Tel: 0870 777 2177 (helpline)

Email: contact@pms.org.uk   **www.pms.org.uk**

Offers members wide variety of services around this problem. Also offers range of free advice and information.

National Osteoporosis Society

Tel: 0845 130 3076 Helpline: 0845 450 0230

Email: info@nos.org.uk   **www.nos.org.uk**

Registered charity which provides help and support for people with osteoporosis and campaigns for greater awareness in the general public, press and medical professions. Supports research.

NHS Direct helpline (24 hours per day)

Tel: 0845 4647

Email: via website   **www.nhsdirect.nhs.uk**

NHS Direct in Scotland: NHS24

Tel: 08454 24 24 24

Email: via website   **www.nhs24.com**

NHS Direct – Wales

Tel: 0845 4647

Email: via website   **www.nhsdirect.wales.nhs.uk**

Positive Action on Cancer

Tel: 01373 455 255

Email: enquiries@positiveactiononcancer.co.uk

www.positiveactiononcancer.co.uk

Free professional one-to-one counselling service for anyone affected by a cancer diagnosis. This includes family, friends and carers as well as cancer patients. Now offers counselling for people bereaved by cancer.

QUIT

National Society of Non-Smokers

Tel: 020 7251 1551   Quitline: 0800 00 22 00

Email: info@quit.org.uk   **www.quit.org.uk**

Information and advice on how to stop smoking.

Release

Tel: 020 7729 5255   Helpline: 0845 4500 215

Email: ask@release.org.uk   **www.release.org.uk**

National agency offering advice, information and counselling for people using drugs – legal or illegal.

Samaritans

Tel: 020 8394 8300   Helpline: 08457 90 90 90

Email: jo@samaritans.org

A telephone support service for those in despair.

Shelter

Helpline: 0808 800 4444

Email: via the websites   England: **www.england.shelter.org.uk**

289

Shelter (continued)   Scotland: **www.scotland.shelter.org.uk**
                                          Wales: **www.cymru.shelter.org.uk**
Charity providing advice and support on housing and the homeless.

The Compassionate Friends
Tel: 0845 120 3785 Helpline: 0845 123 2304
Email: info@tcf.org.uk   **www.tcf.org.uk**
A nationwide self-help organisation of parents whose child of any age, including adult, has died from any cause. Personal and group support. Befriending, not counselling.

Women's Health Concern
Tel: 0845 123 2319
Email: info@womens-health-concern.org

                              www.womens-health-concern.org
Educates and supports women in health issues, especially gynaecological and sexual health.

Women's Sports Foundation
Tel: 020 7273 1740
Email: via website   **www.wsf.org.uk**
The leading national organisation solely committed to improving and promoting opportunities for women in sport.

Women's Therapy Centre
Tel: 020 7263 7860
Email: info@womenstherapycentre.co.uk

                              www.womenstherapycentre.co.uk
Founded in 1976 to provide psychotherapy for women with a feminist perspective. Also offers advice, information, training and publications.

Lesbian Support

Gay's the Word
Tel: 020 7278 7654
Email: sales@gaystheword.co.uk   **www.freespace.virgin.net/gays.theword**
Mail order books – lesbian and gay reading.

Stonewall
Tel: 020 7593 1850

Email: info@stonewall.org.uk   **www.stonewall.org.uk**

Campaign for civil rights for lesbians and gay men.

London Lesbian and Gay Switchboard
Tel: 020 7837 7324

Email: admin@llgs.org.uk   **www.llgs.org.uk**

Nationwide advice service on promoting sexual health and prevention of sexually transmitted diseases.

Queery
Tel: 020 7837 7324   **www.queery.org.uk**

Community-driven directory for Lesbian, Gay, Bisexual & Trans life – online database of services, support groups, events, helplines, resources.

Study and Careers

Ability Net
Tel: 0800 269545

Email: enquiries@abilitynet.org.uk   **www.abilitynet.org.uk**

Organisation to help disabled adults and children use computers and the internet by adapting and adjusting their technology. Runs training courses, offers resources and technical helpline.

CRAC Careers Research and Advisory Centre
Tel: 01223 460277

Email: web.enquiries@crac.org.uk   **www.crac.org.uk**

Promoting lifelong learning and career development. An independent agency and registered charity with 35 years experience of forging links between business and education.

The Federation of Image Consultants
Tel/fax: 07010 701018

Email: info@tfic.org.uk   **www.tfic.org.uk**

Professional body to promote and provide standards for the image industry and personal development industry. Answers enquiries from members of the public about Image Consultants in their area.

Learn Direct

Tel: 0800 100900

Email: via the website **www.learndirect.co.uk**

National helpline providing information and advice on learning, education, training courses with childcare places and funding sources.

The Open University Business School

Tel: 08700 100 311

Email: oubs-ilgen@open.ac.uk **www.oubs.open.ac.uk**

The Open University

Tel: 0845 300 60 90

Email: general-enquiries@open.ac.uk **www.open.ac.uk**

For information on diploma and degree programmes and short courses.

Women's Networks

Business and Professional Women UK Ltd

Tel: 01246 211988

Email: info@bpwuk.co.uk **www.bpwuk.co.uk**

Affiliated with BPW International, which has representation in over 100 countries. Networking, training and development, conferences, social events, campaigning on issues affecting women.

City Women's Network

Tel: 01895 275178

Email: admin@citywomen.org **www.citywomen.org**

Network for professional women – mostly 'city' professions. Provides luncheons, training and acts as a voice for members' views.

Hillcroft College

Tel: 020 8399 2688

Email: enquiry@hillcroft.ac.uk **www.hillcroft.ac.uk**

Registered charity offering range of residential courses for women; specialises in courses for women with few or no qualifications. Free childcare available.

London Women and Manual Trades

Tel: 020 7251 9192

Email: info@wamt.org   **www.wamt.org**

WAMT is the only organisation supporting and advising tradeswomen and women training in the manual trades across the UK. Information on courses, videos, newsletter, list of tradeswomen, survey reports.

National Federation of Women's Institutes

Tel: 020 7371 9300 0

Email: hq@nfwi.org.uk   **www.womens-institute.org.uk**

National Women's Register

Tel: 0845 450 0287

Email: info@nwr.org   **www.nwr.org**

International organisation of women's groups offering opportunities for stimulating discussion of non-domestic nature.

Prowess

Tel: 1603 762355

Email: admin@prowess.org.uk   **www.prowess.org.uk**

A network of organisations and individuals who support the growth of women's business ownership and entrepreneurship. Includes raising awareness, sharing best practice, advocacy and providing information.

The RSA

Tel: 020 7930 5115

Email: general@rsa.org.uk   **www.rsa.org.uk**

Royal Society for the encouragement of Arts, Manufacturers and Commerce. To encourage links with main women's organisations.

SKILL: National Bureau for Students with Disabilities

Tel: 0800 328 5050

Email: info@skill.org.uk   **www.skill.org.uk**

Promoting opportunities for young people and adults with any kind of impairment in post-16 education, training and employment.

Women in Banking and Finance

Tel: 020 8777 6902

Email: admin@wibf.org.uk   **www.wibf.org.uk**

An independent networking group sponsored by banks and other financial organisations run by and for its members. Providing support and a varied calendar of events including training for women working in the financial sector.

Women's Engineering Society

Tel: 01438 765506

Email: info@wes.org.uk   **www.wes.org.uk**

Professional body representing the interests of women engineers.

Women in Management

Tel: 01536 207307

Email: WIM@managers.org.uk   **www.managers.org.uk**

Network of women managers or those planning to be managers. Offers training and development activities and networking groups.

Women in Publishing

Email: info@wipub.org.uk   **www.wipub.org.uk**

Network to provide forum for exchange and support and offer practical training for career and personal development.

Women Returner's Network

Email: via website   **www.women-returners.co.uk**

WRN aims to facilitate the re-entry of women to education, training and employment following a career break. It provides advice and information on training opportunities, free information sheets, a network, quarterly members' newsletter and an annual conference which addresses key themes concerning women's re-entry into the workforce.

Women Welcome Women World Wide

Tel: 01494 465441   www.womenwelcomewomen.org.uk

International network of women offering friendship, correspondence, accommodation.

Working Mothers and Families

Age Concern

Tel: 020 8765 7200 Helpline: 0800 00 99 66   www.ageconcern.org.uk

Network of local Age Concern groups which offers a wide range of support and campaigning activities. Daycentres, support for carers. Information service. Self-help events. Check telephone directory for details of local groups.

Carers UK

Tel: 020 7490 8818

Carers Line: 0808 808 7777 (Weds/Thurs 10am-12 noon & 2-4pm)

Email: info@carersuk.org   www.carersuk.org

Charity to support those whose lives are restricted by caring for sick, disabled and elderly frail relatives and friends. Provides support, information and advice on all aspects of caring. Also lobbies government and other policy makers.

Crysis

Tel: 08451 228 669

Email: info@cry-sis.org.uk   www.cry-sis.org.uk

Support group for parents of excessively crying and/or sleepless babies and young children. Also support for parents of children with behavioural problems e.g. tantrums, clinginess.

Daycare Trust

Tel: 020 7840 3350

Email: info@daycaretrust.org.uk   www.daycaretrust.org.uk

Provides a Hotline information service to employers, parents, nursery staff, trade unions and policy makers. Promotes affordable, accessible and equitable childcare services.

Family Mediators Association

Tel: 0117 117 946 7062 Mediation helpline: 0808 200 0033
Email: via the website   **www.thefma.co.uk**
Helps with family property and financial arrangements when parents/
families split up. Also offers training in the field.

Gingerbread

16-17 Clerkenwell Close, London EC1R 0AA
Tel: 020 7403 9500 Advice line: 0800 018 4318 (9-1pm, Mon-Fri)
Email: office@gingerbread.org.uk   **www.gingerbread.org.uk**
Promotes and supports local self-help groups for one-parent families. Also
provides expert advice and information for lone parents.

Home-Start

Tel: 0116 233 9955
Email: info@home-start.org.uk   **www.home-start.org.uk**
Family support group run by volunteers throughout the UK, supporting
families with at least one child under age of five. Also offers support to
British Forces in Germany and Cyprus.

Hyperactive Children's Support Group

Tel: 01243 539966
Email: hacsg@hacsg.org.uk   **www.hacsg.org.uk**
Supports and advises parents/professionals of hyperactive and ADHD
children using dietary/nutritional therapies. Literature available for sale.

National Childbirth Trust

Tel: 0870 444 8707 (Enquiries) 9.30-4.30
Email: enquiries@nct.org.uk   **www.nct.org.uk**
The NCT offers information and support in pregnancy, childbirth and early
parenthood. Aims to give every parent the chance to make informed
choices. There are over 400 branches throughout the UK.

National Childminding Association

Tel: 0845 880 0044

Email: info@ncma.org.uk   **www.ncma.org.uk**

Membership organisation and charity which provides information, representation and support for registered childminders and parents. Promotes childminding as a quality childcare service. Provides low cost public liability insurance for registered childminders. Free information available.

Parentline Plus

Tel: 020 7284 5500 Helpline: 0808 800 2222

Email: via the website   **www.parentlineplus.org.uk**

Freephone helpline for anyone caring for a child. Emotional support, information, the chance to talk through problems in confidence.

Relate

Tel: 0845 456 1310

Email: via the website   **www.relate.org.uk**

Provides counselling for adults with relationship problems through 600 locations in England, Wales and Northern Ireland.

Stillbirth and Neonatal Death Society

Tel: 020 7436 7940 Helpline: 020 7436 5881

Email: support@uk-sands.org   **www.uk-sands.org**

SANDS provides support for bereaved parents and their families when their baby dies at or soon after birth. National telephone helpline service; UK-wide network of local self-help groups; information and publications for bereaved parents and professionals.

Women's Aid

Tel: 0117 944 4411 Helpline: 0808 2000 247

Email: info@womensaid.org.uk   **www.womensaid.org.uk**

Helps women and children who are experiencing violence in the home.

Books

This is not a definitive list but will get you off to a good start:

Other books by the Authors of this book

Liz Willis and Jenny Daisley – *Developing Women through Training* – The Springboard Consultancy – 2006
A practical how-to-do-it guide on women's development training. Written for organisations and women's groups.

Jenny Daisley and Liz Willis – *Women Singled Out* – The Springboard Consultancy – 1995
Research report on why single gender training works.

Liz Willis and Jenny Daisley – *Personal Development has Legs* – The Springboard Consultancy – 2006
Research report on the longer term benefits of the Springboard Women's Development Programme and other programmes run by the Consultancy.

Liz Willis and Jenny Daisley – *The Assertive Trainer* – The Springboard Consultancy – 1994
A practical guide for trainers on their use of assertiveness.

Assertiveness

Ken and Kate Back – *Assertiveness at Work* – McGraw Hill – 2005
Considered by some to be the definitive book on assertiveness at work. Useful background reading.

Anne Dickson – *A Woman in your Own Right* – Quartet – 2002
Basic guide to assertion with emphasis on techniques – revised and updated.

Adrian Furnham – *Body Language at Work* – Chartered Institute of Personnel and Development – 1999

Gael Lindenfield – *Assert Yourself* – Thorsons – 2001
How to develop assertiveness and build confidence.

Susan Newman – *The Book of No* – McGraw Hill – 2006
Overscheduled? Overworked? Overburdened? Get the 'no how' you need to take back your life.

Allan and Barbara Pease – *The Definitive Book of Body Language* – Orion– 2005
People's body language often reveals that what they say is very different from what they think or feel.

Disability Issues

AA – *Disabled Traveller's Guide* – 2004
Comprehensive guide for disabled travellers, including new section aimed at older drivers, and travelling without a car. Free download from AA.

Maggie Black and Penny Gray – *Coping with RSI* – Sheldon Press – 1999
How to cope with Repetitive Strain Injury.

Darnborough and Kinrade – *Directory for Disabled People* – Prentice Hall – 1998
Handbook of information and opportunities for disabled people.

Ian Greaves – *Disability Rights Handbook 2006* – Disability Alliance Educational and Research Association
Updated annually, the handbook is acknowledged as the most comprehensive reference guide to benefits and services for all disabled people, their families, carers and advisers.

Gerald Hales (ed) – *Beyond Disability* – Sage Publications Ltd – 1995
A study of how society intervenes in the lives of people with disabilities, with contributors exploring how resources for 'disabled' individuals could be used more effectively.

Michael Oliver – *Understanding Disability* – Palgrave Macmillan– 1995
This book is useful and enlightening to disabled and non-disabled people alike. A valuable contribution to debates about our understanding of disability and the position of disabled people in society.

Carol Thomas – *Female Forms* – Open University Press – 1999
This work explores and develops ideas about disability. The title 'Female Forms' reflects two things: first, disabled women's experiences, as told by themselves; and second, the author's belief in the importance of feminist ideas and debates for disability studies.

Michele Wates and Rowen Jade (eds) – *Bigger Than the Sky – Disabled Women on Parenting* – The Women's Press – 1999
Anthology exploring parenting and disability from diverse perspectives. Challenges restrictive definitions and celebrates difference.

Health

Jeanne Achterberg – *Woman as Healer* – Shambhala Publications - 1991
The healing activities of women from prehistoric times to now.

Anne Dickson and Nikki Henriques – *Hysterectomy: the Woman's View* – Quartet – 1994
Demystifies the facts around hysterectomy and describes women's experiences.

Germaine Greer – *The Change* – Random House – 1994
Women, ageing and the menopause.

Louise Hay – *You can Heal your Life* – Hay House – 2004
The powerful effect of positive thinking on your health and well-being.

Nick Heather and Ian Robertson – *Problem Drinking* – Oxford University Press (Third Edition) – 1997
Argues that 'alcoholism' is best viewed as a learned behavioural disorder rather than a disease. Aims to bridge the gap between popular views and the modern scientific understanding.

Leslie Kenton – *Passage to Power* – Vermilion – 1998
Brilliant book on natural ways of living through the menopause.

Caroline Myss – *Why People Don't Heal and How They Can* –
Bantam Books – 1998
Looks at health and healing in a spiritual and holistic context.

Dr Christiane Northrup – *Women's Bodies, Women's Wisdom* – Piatkus –
2004
*Informative guide to all aspects of holistic health and well-being for
women. Explains how the female body works, how women can take
control of their own healing. Includes many real-life stories.*

Rosamond Richardson – *Natural Superwoman* – Kyle Cathie – 2003
*The Survival Guide for women who have too much to do. Covers your
living space, relationships, eating well, finding me-time.*

Chris Stevens – *The Alexander Technique* – Vermilion – 1996
Light, easily readable introduction.

Dr Miriam Stoppard – *Well Woman* – Dorling Kindersley – 1998
*Mini encyclopaedia of health issues relating to women. Covers symptoms,
what a doctor will do, plus suggestions for complementary therapies.*

Michael van Straten – *Superjuice – Juicing for Health and Healing* –
Mitchell Beazley – 2004
*Not only full of fantastic recipes but van Straten describes which vitamins
and minerals are contained in the all the fruit and vegetables ingredients
used in the recipes. In "Drink yourself better" tables he provides an easy-
to-use directory of common ailments – along with which juices you should
drink to heal them.*
*(A personal recommendation from C Wilson – apple, carrot and beetroot –
heavenly and earthy at the same time!)*

Personal Development

Stephen Baylery and Roger Mavity – *Life's a Pitch* – 2007
How to be businesslike with your emotional life and emotional with your business life.

Richard Bolles – *What Color is your Parachute?* – Ten Speed Press – 2005
A practical manual for job hunters and career changers. Excellent. Crammed with inspiration, information and lots of practical exercises.

Edward de Bono – *de Bono's Thinking Course* – BBC Active– 2006
De Bono demonstrates how the techniques of thinking can be enhanced and improved through attention, practice and the use of simple tools, such as lateral thinking and goal setting.

John Bradshaw – *Homecoming* – Piatkus – 2004
Healing and transforming your life by 'reclaiming and championing your inner child.'

Dr Gilbert Childs – *Understand YOUR Temperament!* – Sophia Books – 1995
Fascinating contemporary account of the ancient doctrine of the four temperaments. How to recognise and understand the temperaments in yourself and others.

Petruska Clarkson – *The Achilles Syndrome* – Element – 1998
Identifies the secret fear of failure felt by many apparently successful people. Explains the reasons and how to resolve the feelings of never being good enough.

Stephen R Covey – *The Seven Habits of Highly Effective People* – Simon and Schuster – 2004
Powerful lessons on personal change.

Jinny S Ditzler – *Your Best Year Yet!* – Harper Element – 2006
Simple 10-question process designed to clarify personal values, dreams and ambitions into achievable goals and an action plan for change.

Lynda Field – *Self Esteem for Women* – Vermilion – 2001
Building a positive self-image and maintaining high self-esteem.

Thomas A Harris – *I'm OK, You're OK* – Arrow – 1995
*The classic description of Transactional Analysis. Has links with
Assertiveness.*

Amy Harris and Thomas Harris – *Staying OK* – Arrow – 1995
The popular sequel to I'm OK, You're OK.

Louise L Hay – *Empowering Women* – Hodder Mobius – 1998
*All-round self-help, from self-esteem to family life, health, sexuality and
improving your quality of life.*

Louise Hay – *The Power is Within You* – Hay House – 2002
*How to overcome the emotional barriers we place in our own paths and
reprogramme our headtapes to be more positive.*

Susan Jeffers – *Feel the Fear and Do It Anyway* – Vermilion – 2007
*A recommended classic – how to turn your fear and indecision into
confidence and action.*

Susan Jeffers – *Feel the Fear and Beyond* – Rider Books – 2000
Filled with exercises to teach you that you can handle what life brings.

Susan Jeffers – *End the Struggle and Dance with Life* – Hodder and
Stoughton – 2005
How to build yourself up when the world gets you down – very uplifting.

Gael Lindenfield – *The Positive Woman* – Thorsons Element– 2000
Positive and woman together – ways to make it happen.

Lia Macko and Kerry Rubin – *Midlife Crisis at 30; Turning your Inevitable
Meltdown into the Life you really Want* – Rodale Books – 2004
*Reveals that many 20- and 30-something women have distorted, well-
intentioned empowerment messages and they are blaming themselves*

when they fail to overcome the very real obstacles that still exist... gives solutions.

Fiona Parashar – *The Balancing Act* – Simon & Schuster – 2003
Work-life solutions for busy people.

Verna Peiffer – *Banish Bad Habits Forever* – Piatkus – 2005
Increase your confidence and achieve your goals.

Anne Wilson Schaef – *Meditations for Women who Do Too Much* – Harper San Francisco – 2004
For all of us who do too much – a thought for every day – warm and perceptive. Required reading for workaholics and careaholics!

Neale Donald Walsch – *The Little Soul and the Sun* – Hampton Roads Publishing Company, Inc. – 1998
Illustrated children's parable adapted from 'Conversations with God'.

Relationships

Steve Biddulph – *Manhood* – Vermilion – 2004
Full of personal experiences, insights and practical advice for changing men's lives. For women who want to understand what helps and hinders men's development as sons, partners or fathers.

Steve Biddulph – *The Secret of Happy Children* – Thorsons – 1999
Practical parenting advice covering parent-child communication, curing tantrums, shyness and whinging, making life easier as a single parent, how to be more relaxed and effective with your children.

Robert Bly – *Iron John* – Rider & Co – 2001
The much discussed book about men, possibly pioneering a new interest in men's development.

Deborah Cameron – *Verbal Hygiene* – Routledge – 2004
Popular attitudes towards language and the practices by which people try

to regulate its use. Interesting chapters on political correctness, including non-sexist language, and on old and new ideas about language and gender, including current self-help advice aimed at women speakers.

Susan Faludi – *Stiffed – The Betrayal of the Modern Man* – Vintage – 2000
Follow-up to Backlash *(a famous feminist book), this explores the position of men in the wake of feminism.*

John Gray – *Men are from Mars, Women are from Venus* – Harper Element – 2003
A practical guide to relationships between men and women.

Sam Keen – *Fire in the Belly* – Bantam USA – 1992
One of the wave of books helping to find a new identity for men in today's world.

Harriet Goldhor Lerner – *The Dance of Intimacy: a Woman's Guide to Courageous Acts of Change in Key Relationships* – HarperPerennial – 2003
This guide outlines the steps women can take to strengthen good relationships and heal difficult ones.

Florence Littauer – *Personality Plus* – Monarch Publications – 1995
'The key to understanding others lies in understanding yourself'. How your personality affects your emotions, work and relationships, how to bring out the best in yourself and others.

Sarah Litvinoff – *The Relate Guide to Better Relationships* – Vermilion – 2001

Robin Norwood – *Women who Love Too Much* – Arrow Books – 2004
For the woman who loves men who don't love back. Recommended.

Dr Linda Papadopoulos – *The man manual* – Hodder and Stroughton – 2005.
Everything you've ever wanted to know about your man and probably things you didn't want to know too.

Allan and Barbara Pease – *Why Men Don't Listen & Women Can't Read Maps* – Orion – 2004
Looks at how men and women are different – and what to do about it.

Victoria Secunda – *When You and Your Mother can't Be Friends* – Delta – 1991
An eye-opener. Explains the difficulties in the mother/daughter relationship and offers practical advice to help heal and let go.

Judith R Smith – *Time to Fly Free: Meditations for those who have left an Abusive Relationship* – Hazelden – 2001
A guide for survivors of abusive relationships... offers daily inspiration and gentle guidance that addresses self-esteem, managing painful emotions, rediscovering sexuality and avoiding future abusive relationships.

Deborah Tannen – *You Just Don't Understand* – Virago – 2002
A real eye-opener. Identifies the different ways in which men and women use conversation and explains why there are so many misunderstandings in our communications.

Deborah Tannen – *That's Not What I Meant!* – Virago – 2003
How conversational style makes or breaks your relationships with others.

Deborah Tannen – *The Argument Culture* – Virago – 1999
How adversarial modes of debate often prevent clear communication in public life. The role of gender, what we can learn from other cultures, how we might change the way we debate and argue.

Sexuality

Amity Pierce Buxton – *The Other Side of the Closet* – John Wiley & Sons – 1994
This is a compassionate and candid look at an untold chapter of gay liberation – the crisis that ensues when a parent or partner reveals their homosexuality. Based on hundreds of interviews conducted over seven years, the guide includes information for children and family members.

Anne Dickson – *The Mirror Within* – Quartet – 2001
A new look at sexuality for women.

Richard A MacKey, Bernard A O'Brien and Eileen F MacKey – *Gay and Lesbian Couples* – Greenwood Press – 1997
Based on interviews with gay couples in long-term relationships, this book focuses on how partners worked out their roles, the nature of relational fit between them, conflict management, social supports, and change and psychological intimacy over the years.

Angela Mason and Anya Palmer – *Queer Bashing* – Stonewall – 1996
Survey report and personal stories of the violence and harassment experienced by lesbians and gay men in the UK – horrifying and sobering reading.

Rich Rasi (ed) – *Out in the Workplace, the Perils and Pleasures of Coming Out on the Job* – Alyson Publications – 1996
Worth reading for lesbian and informative for heterosexual women.

Skills

John Lees – *How to get the job you love* – McGraw Hill – 2007
A must for checking out how to write applications, CVs and covering letters and emails.

Andrew Leigh – *The Ultimate Presentation Book* – Random House – 1999
Large paperback, covering all aspects of presentations, from layouts of rooms to attitudes and approaches. Very readable and practical, with various A-Z sections.

Elisa Lottor and Nancy Bruning – *Female and Forgetful: A 6-Step Program to Restore your Memory* – Little, Brown – 2002
Millions of women, ranging from mid-30s to 50s and beyond, experience lapses in memory: misplacing keys, losing their train of thought mid-sentence, walking into a room and forgetting why. Explanations and solutions.

Thich Nhat Hanh – *Calming the Fearful Mind* – Parallax Press – 2005
This book reveals the secrets to liberating ourselves from fear particularly in an age of terror and terrorism.

Barbara Killinger – *Workaholics, the Respectable Addicts* – Key Porter Books – 2004
By far the best and most helpful book on workaholism with practical strategies for recovery.

Bonnie C McKenzie – *Friends in High Places* – Allen & Unwin – 1995
Written by a Springboard trainer. Lots of hints and tips on finding and making the most of a mentor.

Gabrielle Mander – *What emails say about you* – Virgin Books Ltd – 2006
A humorous self-analysis book, which tells us how and when we use emails and what they give away.

Casey Miller and Kate Swift – *The Handbook of Non-sexist Writing for Writers, Editors and Speakers* – The Women's Press – 1995

Dale Spender – *Nattering on the Net* – Spinifex – 1996
Great book explaining how the Internet works and the importance of women getting involved.

Deborah Tannen – *Talking from 9 to 5* – Virago – 1996
Men and women at work – who gets heard and who gets credit for work done.

Judith C Tingley and Lee E Robert – *Gendersell* – Simon & Shuster – 2000
Presents very interesting research about selling to and working with the opposite sex. Deals with each separately, offers practical tips to use in the workplace.

Carol Vorderman – *Super Brain* – Vermilion – 2007
101 Easy ways to a more agile mind – a mixture of old favourites and new brain teasers.

Lucy Martin and Bella Mehta – *Make it Your Business* – Springhill – 2006
A good upbeat checklist of both practical information and the mindset required to strike out alone or with others.

Women's Issues

Maya Angelou – *I Know Why the Caged Bird Sings* – Virago – 2003
Very powerful autobiographical account of a black woman growing up.

Clare Brant and Yun Lee Too – *Rethinking Sexual Harassment* – Pluto Press – 1994
Selection of essays from a wide range of perspectives.

Charlotte Cole and Helen Windrath (eds) – *The Female Odyssey* – The Women's Press – 1999
Wide-ranging essays by leading women writers and activists from around the world. Where women stand today and their hopes and visions for the future.

Stuart Crainer – *Key Management Ideas* – FT/Prentice Hall – 1998
Gives you fast and focused insight into the most important management ideas of our time.

Judith Duerk – *Circle of Stones: Woman's Journey to Herself* – Innisfree Press – 2004
Draws the reader into a meditative experience of the lost Feminine and creates a space for us to consider our present lives from the eyes of women's ancient culture and ritual.

EOC – *Facts about Women and Men in Great Britain* – 2006
*Free pdf download, packed with the facts about how we live our lives.
Go to www.eoc.org.uk and search for the title in 'Publications'.
Note: from October 2007 the EOC is part of the CEHR. www.cehr.org.uk*

Susan Faludi – *Backlash* – Vintage – 1993
The prize-winning and controversial assessment of the effect of feminism. Much talked about.

Evelyn Fazio and Pam Brodowsky – *Staying Sane when Going Through the Menopause* – Da Capo Press – 2007
Here's how other savvy, sexy women have tamed the mid-life demons and stayed lean, even-keeled and in charge of 'The Change'. Includes practical tips and coping strategies.

Margaret Flanders – *Breakthrough* – Sage – 1994
Practical guide for career women on shattering the 'glass ceiling'.

Lois P Frankel – *Nice Girls don't get the Corner Office: 101 Unconscious Mistakes Women make* – Little, Brown – 2005
From executive to entry level, every woman needs to know what she is doing to subconsciously sound, look, act, market herself, and/or be treated like a 'girl'. This book will help women to become aware of when and how they are damaging their careers and will give the advice and tips they need to help replace these self-defeating behaviours with more effective ones.

Candice Fredrick, Camille Atkinson – *Women, Ethics and the Workplace* – Greenwood Press – 1997
Since women are entering the workforce in record numbers, there is an urgency to address specific ethical problems with which they are faced. The authors focus on sexual harassment, comparable worth, leadership, advertising, and working-class women.

Suzanne Braun Levine – *The Woman's Guide to Second Adulthood: Inventing the Rest of our Lives* – Bloomsbury – 2006
The first generation of socially emancipated women have fulfilled all their roles: daughter, wife, mother, career woman. (Levine) raises three crucial questions that each woman must answer for herself: What matters? What works? What's next? Drawing on interviews, science, trend analysis and loads of case studies.

Jennifer Louden – *Comfort Secrets for Busy Women – Finding your Way when your Life is Overflowing* – Sourcebooks – 2006
Filled with questions that provide women with an access to their inner

voice, along with reflection on how to bring comfort and peace into even the most stressful lives.

Robin McGraw – *Inside my Heart: Choosing to Live with Passion and Purpose* – Nelson Books – 2007
Aims to speak directly to the heart of every woman and challenges her to recognise and lead her to her unique role to lead her to satisfaction with herself, her profession, her family and anything she strives for.

Vickie Milazzo – *Inside Every Woman: Using the Ten Strengths you didn't know you had to get the Career and Life you want Now* – John Wiley – 2006
A self-made millionaire entrepreneur shows women how to get ahead using the inner strengths all women possess... Vickie encourages women to employ their feminine forces such as intuitive vision, agility and endurance to transform their lives.

Zana Muhsen with Andrew Crofts – *SOLD* – Time Warner– 2004
Story of Birmingham-born Zana Muhsen, sold into marriage in the Yemen, and her courageous fight for freedom.

Vrinda Nabar – *Caste As Woman* – Penguin Books – 2003
The Indian woman today, from girl-child to widowhood. Examines the influences of caste, gender and cultural and historical conditioning.

Miriam E Nelson – *Strong Women Stay Young* – Aurum Press – 2000
The scientifically-proven strength training programme that burns back the clock – replacing fat with muscle, reversing bone loss, increasing strength and energy – all in just two at-home sessions per week.

Susan Nolen-Hoeksema – *Women who Think too Much: how to Break Free of Over-thinking and Reclaim your Life* – Piatkus – 2004
Previously psychologists encouraged the view that constantly analysing and expressing our emotions is a good thing. This book challenges this assumption, discusses why women are particularly prone to negative thinking, offers techniques for overcoming over-thinking and finds real solutions to problems.

Susie Orbach – *Fat is a Feminist Issue* – Arrow – 2006
About 'fattist' attitudes, media representation, diets and the perception of what it is to be 'fat'.

Ruth Picardie – *Before I Say Goodbye* – Penguin – 1998
Collection of correspondence and thoughts from Ruth Picardie, dying from breast cancer, and her family.

Dale Spender – *Man Made Language* – Rivers Oram Press – 1998
The definitive book on the way our language devalues women. Good awareness-raising stuff.

Jennifer Uglow (ed) revised by Maggy Hendry (ed, 4th edition) – *The Palgrave Macmillan Dictionary of Women's Biography* – Palgrave Macmillan – 2005
The lives and achievements of over 2000 remarkable women, from ancient times to the present day. Excellent reference book.

Some CDs

Relaxations from the Springboard Consultancy
Three tracks of relaxations and visualisations by Jenny Daisley, co-author of the Springboard Women's Development Workbook.
Tel: 01271 850 828 Email: office@springboardconsultancy.com

'Letting go'
Marie McStay (Springboard and Spring Forward trainer in Ireland)
Two tracks; one giving clear instructions for relaxation and the other is visualisation for helping let go of negativity. Available directly from Marie.
Tel: 028 4173 8624 Email: mcstaym@aol.com

Useful Websites

Websites are constantly changing so here are a few to get you started or to add to your list of favourites. Organisations in the earlier part of the chapter have their websites given there.

www.springboardconsultancy.com
All about the consultancy and its work worldwide.

www.city-and-guilds.co.uk
To find out more about qualifications.

www.dfes.gov.uk
To find out what is happening in the world of education and training – up-to-date information on what is available.

www.disabilityalliance.org
The Disability Alliance website.

www.drc-gb.org
Disability Rights Commission website.

www.jobsguardian.co.uk
The Guardian newspaper's site for job seekers. Browse vacancies by sector or search for specific job titles.

www.mslexia.co.uk
A Springboard participant really took off with her creative writing during the course and recommends [this] website and magazine for women who want to write and possibly get in print.

www.patient.co.uk
Provides accessible medical information. Alphabetical listing covers very wide choice of subjects/problems, including many on women's health issues from anorexia to the menopause.

www.planetgrrl.com

For UK women and girls. Relationships, jobs, health, ecology, the internet and much more.

www.positivepress.com

For good news and positive sayings.

www.womenandequalityunit.gov.uk

Information on women's ministers, policies, and fact sheets on topics like family friendly employment.

www.womenconnect.org.uk

UK based internet networking project for women's groups and organisations.

www.wowwomen.com

Celebrating the spirit of womankind.

www.allaboutyou.com

Lifestyle and advice.

www.handbag.com

Magazine and lifestyle.

www.campaign-for-learning.org.uk

Encourages family and workplace learning.

www.basic-skills.co.uk

Agency supporting people of all ages who struggle with words and numbers.

www.move-on.org.uk

Promoting improvement of numeracy and literacy skills and gaining qualifications for the workplace.

www.niace.org.uk

Promotes adult continuing education.

www.bbc.co.uk/skillswise
To improve English and Maths.

www.bbc.co.uk/learning/
Online learning, support and advice.

www.bbc.co.uk/raw
Campaign to improve reading and writing.

www.thewomenscompany.com
Networking lunches and other events.

www.pansophix.com/
Commercial training company offering selection of free resources on professional and personal development.

www.pinknews.co.uk
Gay news in the UK and further afield.

www.freecycle.org
Fast growing international network of local groups who promote waste reduction by free 'getting-and-giving' of wide variety of items.

www.wen.org
Women's Environmental Network campaigns on environment and health from a female perspective.

http://petitions.pm.gov.uk
Create and add to e-petitions sent direct to Prime Minister on wide range of subjects.

www.un.org/womenwatch/daw
Division for the Advancement of Women gives overview of UN action globally.

www.emptyclosets.com
Resources and supportive chat forum for coming out.

Index

Other Books from Hawthorn Press

320pp; 297 x 210mm;
paperback; 978-1-903458-61-7

Navigator (2nd edition)
Men's development workbook
James Traeger, Jenny Daisley, Liz Willis

Life for men is changing. Employment patterns, job security, women's roles and other social patterns continue to change rapidly. Many men are asking who they are and how they can not only survive but thrive amongst these changes.

The Navigator workbook is packed with ideas and practical exercises to enable you to assess yourself realistically, identify where you want to go in life and then equip you with the positive attitude and many of the skills you may need to get there.

Between Form and Freedom
(Second Edition)
Being a Teenager
Betty Staley

Between Form and Freedom has a wealth of helpful insights about teenagers, offering a wise look into the souls of children and adolescents. Betty Staley invites you to explore the vibrant nature of adolescence- the search for the self, the birth of the intellect, the release of feeling, male–female differences and character.

288pp; 216 × 138mm
paperback; 978-1-903458-89-1

320pp; 234 × 156mm;
paperback; 978-1-903458-78-5

Healing Stories
for Challenging Behaviour
Susan Perrow

Susan Perrow is a story doctor who writes and collects stories that offer a therapeutic journey for the storyteller and listener – a positive, imaginative way of healing difficult situations. Here are stories for helping a range of common childhood issues such as separation anxiety, bullying, sibling rivalry, and nightmares and grieving. There is a guide for creating healing stories, as well as a comprehensive collection of stories with note and suggestions for use.

Orders

If you have difficulties ordering Hawthorn Press books from a bookshop, you can order direct from:

Booksource
50 Cambuslang Road, Glasgow, G32 8NB
Tel: (0845) 370 0063
Fax: (0845) 370 0064
E-mail: orders@booksource.net

Further information/Book catalogue

Hawthorn Press
1 Lansdown Lane, Stroud
Gloucestershire, GL5 1BJ, UK
Tel: +(44) (0) 1453 757040
Fax: +(44) (0) 1453 751138
E-mail: info@hawthornpress.com
Website: www.hawthornpress.com

Dear Reader

If you wish to follow up your reading of this book, please tick the boxes below as appropriate, fill in your name and address and return to Hawthorn Press:

☐ Please send me a catalogue of other Hawthorn Press books.

☐ Please send me details of Personal Development events and courses.

My feedback about Personal Development:

Name _____

Address _____

_____

_____

Postcode _____ Tel no _____

Please return to:
Hawthorn Press, Hawthorn House, 1 Lansdown Lane,
Stroud, Glos. GL5 1BJ, UK

or Fax (01453) 751135

SPB 2007